Longman

Contents

Miscellany

Poetry

The short story

Playscripts

□ This symbol links a question with a picture.

MISCELLANY

1 Information

One of the main uses of language is to pass on information.

We can see language being used for this purpose in reference books and on cornflake packets, tins of food and road signs.

It is this language of information, advice and instruction that we look at in the pages that follow.

Information can also be passed on in the form of diagrams, maps and figures, and examples of these are also given.

Contents

Dictionaries

A dictionary contains a lot of information.

Apart from the spelling, meaning and pronunciation of words there may be maps, diagrams and drawings to show what persons, places and things look like.

Below and on page 4 are two pages from the *Longman New Generation Dictionary*. One uses a drawing to give information and the other uses words.

Look first at the drawing and then answer the questions.

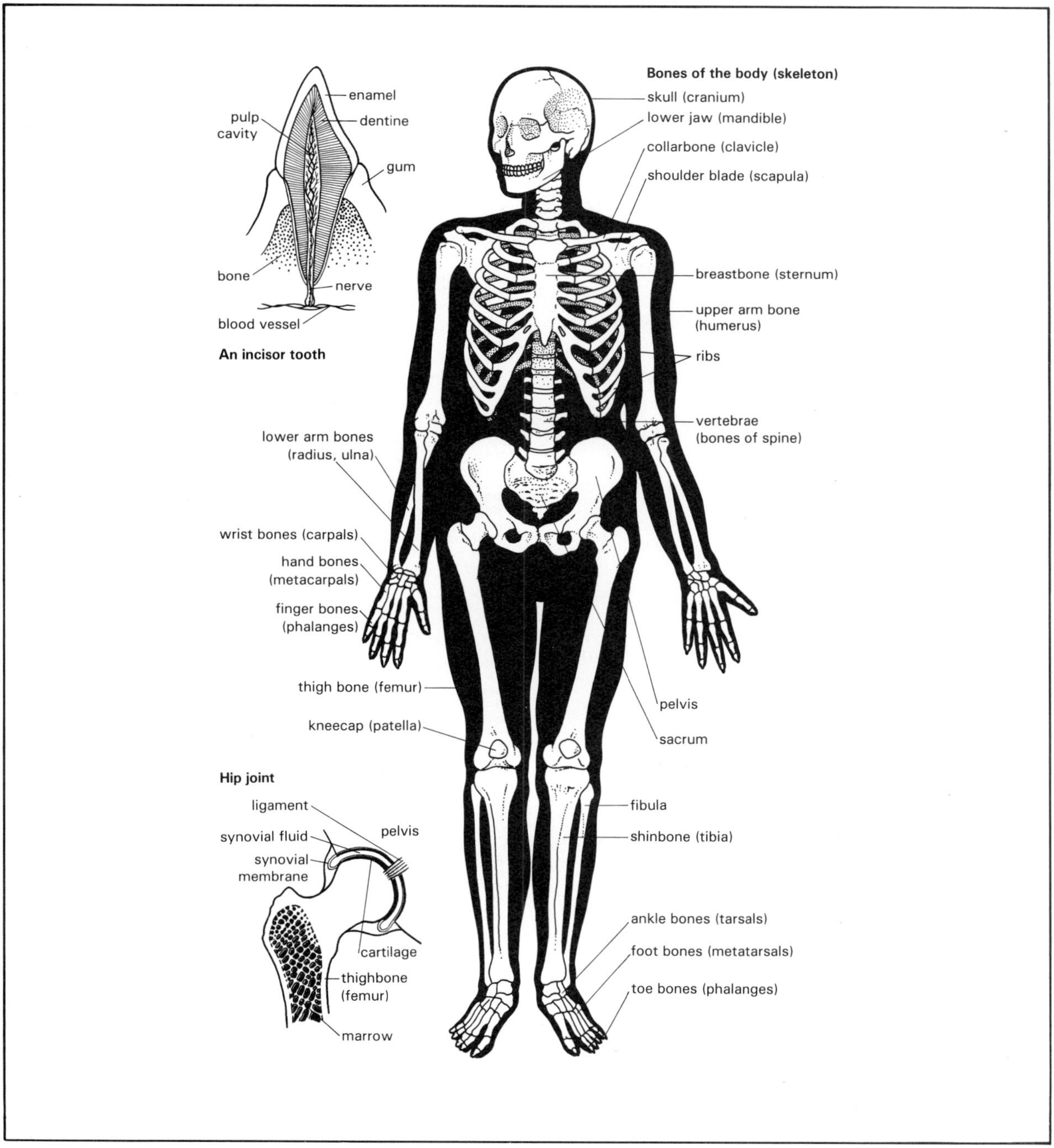

Questions to answer

1 Where are the *radius* and the *ulna*?
2 What is the difference between a *metacarpal* and a *metatarsal*?
3 Describe in your own words the shape of the *pelvis*.
4 Is the *humerus* your 'funny bone'?
5 In the *hip joint* there is a fluid that helps the ball of the *femur* turn in the socket of the *pelvis*. What is that fluid called?
6 Here are some lines from a poem called *Dry Bones*.

With your toe bone connected to your foot bone,
Your foot bone connected to your heel bone,
Your heel bone connected to your ankle bone,
Your ankle bone connected to your leg bone,
Your leg bone connected to your knee bone,
Your knee bone connected to your thigh bone,
Your thigh bone connected to your hip bone,
Your hip bone connected to your back bone,
Your back bone connected to your shoulder bone,
Your shoulder bone connected to your neck bone,
Your neck bone connected to your head bone,
Now hear the Word of the Lord.

Write them out but this time give where possible the correct name for each bone, e.g.

With your phalange connected to your metatarsal

7 What lies between the *enamel* of a tooth and its *pulp cavity*?
8 Where would one find *marrow*?
9 What are *vertebrae*?
10 Is the *sternum* at the back or the front of the skeleton?

Here is another page from the same dictionary. Notice two things:

- all the words are in alphabetical order
- when a lot of words begin with the same letters we have to go deeper and deeper into the word to find the alphabetical order

107 **che**

charisma *n* **-mas** *or* **-mata** great personal charm which gives the power to influence others — **~tic** *adj* — **~tically** *adv*
charitable *adj* full of goodness; forgiving; generous; concerned with the poor: *a charitable club* — **-bly** *adv*
charity *n* **-ties** 1 the giving of help to the poor 2 an organization that gives this help 3 **charity begins at home** one's first duty is to one's family 4 **(as) cold as charity** unfeeling; unfriendly
charlatan *n* *offensive* a person who falsely claims to have (usu. medical) knowledge or skill —compare QUACK
Charleston *n* a lively dance, esp. popular in the 1920's
charlotte *n* a dish made of layers of (usu.) apple and of breadcrumbs
charm[1] *n* 1 a magic word or act 2 an object worn to keep away evil or bring luck 3 the power or ability to please or win over 4 **work like a charm** *esp. spoken* to be a complete success
charm[2] *v* 1 to please; win over; delight 2 to control or protect (something) as if by magic — **~er** *n* — **~ing** *adj* — **~ingly** *adv*
chart[1] *n* 1 a map, esp. a detailed map of a sea area 2 (a sheet of paper with) information in written or illustrated form: *weather chart*
chart[2] *v* 1 to make a map or chart of 2 *esp. spoken* to make a rough plan, in writing
charter[1] *n* 1 an official document giving rights, freedoms, etc. 2 the practice of hiring or renting buses, planes, etc.: *charter flights*
charter[2] *v* to hire or rent (a plane, bus, etc.)
chartered accountant *n* an accountant who has full professional recognition
charwoman also **charlady, char—** *n* **charwomen** a woman who works as a cleaner
chary *adj* **-ier, -iest** careful; cautious — **charily** *adv*
Charybdis *n* see SCYLLA
chase[1] *v* **chased, chasing** to run after; to hunt; to drive away
chase[2] *n* 1 an act of chasing 2 **give chase** to chase
chase[3] *v* *technical* to engrave wood or metal — **~r** *n*
chaser *n* a weaker alcoholic drink drunk after a stronger one
chasm *n* a very deep crack or opening in the earth or ice
chassis *n* **chassis** 1 the framework on which the body and working parts of a vehicle, radio, etc. are fastened or built 2 the frame and working parts of a car, radio, etc. as opposed to its body 3 the landing apparatus of a plane
chaste *adj* 1 pure in word, thought, and deed, esp. sexually pure 2 simple: *He wrote in a chaste style* — **~ly** *adv*
chasten *v* to correct by punishment; purify; cause (a person or behaviour) to improve
chastise *v* **-tised, -tising** *esp. written* to punish severely, usu. by beating — **~ment** *n*
chastity *n* the state of being sexually pure —compare CELIBACY
chat[1] *v* *esp. spoken* to talk in a friendly manner
chat[2] *n* *esp. spoken* a gossipy conversation
château, chat- *n* **-teaus** *or* **-teaux** *French* a castle or large country house in France
chattel *n* *law* an article of movable property (esp. in the phrase **goods and chattels**)
chatter[1] *v* 1 to talk rapidly and idly at length- 2 (of certain animals and birds) to make rapid speechlike sounds 3 to knock together, esp. through cold or fear — **~er** *n*
chatter[2] *n* 1 rapid small talk 2 a rapid knocking sound made by teeth, machines, etc.
chatterbox *n* *esp. spoken* a talkative person, esp. a child
chatty *adj* **-tier, tiest** *esp. spoken* talkative
chat up *v adv* *esp. spoken* (esp. of men) to make friends with by talking to (esp. a woman)
chauffeur[1] *n* a person employed to drive someone's car
chauffeur[2] *v* to act as driver for (a person)
chauvinism *n* unreasoned belief in the superiority of one's own nation, group, or sex to any other: *male chauvinism* — **-ist** *n, adj* — **-istic** *adj* — **-istically** *adv*
cheap[1] *n* **on the cheap** *esp. spoken* without paying the full cost
cheap[2] *adj* 1 low in price; good value 2 charging low prices —opposite **expensive** 3 needing little effort: *The army won a cheap victory* 4 worth little 5 **a** of poor quality; shoddy **b** vulgar 6 **dirt cheap** *esp. spoken* at a very low price 7 **feel cheap** *esp. spoken* to feel ashamed — **~ly** *adv* — **~ness** *n*
cheapen *v* to make or become cheaper in price or value
cheap-jack *adj* of bad quality
cheat[1] *n* 1 a dishonest person 2 an example of cheating; deceitful trick 3 a card game in which 2 or more players try to win by cheating
cheat[2] *v* 1 to trick (someone) 2 to act dishonestly or deceitfully to win an advantage, esp. in a game 3 to escape as if by deception: *The swimmers cheated death in spite of the storm*
check[1] *n* 1 a stop; control: *We've kept the disease in check for a year now* 2 something which stops, controls, etc. 3 an examination to make certain that something is correct 4 a standard against which something can be examined 5 a receipt; ticket or object for claiming something 6 a pattern of squares 7 the position of the king in chess when under direct attack
check[2] *v* 1 to stop; control; hold back 2 to test, examine, or mark to see if correct
checked *adj* having a pattern of squares
checkers *n* *US* draughts
check in *v adv* to report one's arrival, as at an airport
checkmate[1] *v* **-mated, -mating** 1 to win a game of chess by preventing the opponent's king from being moved 2 to stop; completely defeat

We can see this more clearly by looking at the first six words:

charisma *n* **-mas** *or* **-mata** great personal charm which gives the power to influence others — **~tic** *adj* — **~tically** *adv*
charitable *adj* full of goodness; forgiving; generous; concerned with the poor: *a charitable club* — **-bly** *adv*
charity *n* **-ties** **1** the giving of help to the poor **2** an organization that gives this help **3** **charity begins at home** one's first duty is to one's family **4** **(as) cold as charity** unfeeling; unfriendly
charlatan *n* *offensive* a person who falsely claims to have (usu. medical) knowledge or skill —compare QUACK
Charleston *n* a lively dance, esp. popular in the 1920's
charlotte *n* a dish made of layers of (usu.) apple and of breadcrumbs

They are in this order on the page because:

- all begin with CHAR
- fifth letters are used to place words beginning with CHARI in alphabetical order before those beginning with CHARL
- sixth, seventh, eighth, ninth and tenth letters of words are then used to get them into a final alphabetical order

Here are some words for *you* to put in alphabetical order.

swarm nod here fence plum
wipe knife orange egg x-ray
bell man tea car very
yellow day game jam ran

Now look at the second letter of these words beginning with *f* and put those in alphabetical order.

fuel face fog felt frank flea
field

All the following words have the same first and second letters. Can you group them by their third letters?

fame fable fake fair fade
faggot false

A difficult one with which to finish. These words all begin with *fl*. Put them in alphabetical order.

fleck flatten flaw flea flavour
flax flatter flay flask flash

Questions to answer

Use page 4 to help you answer the following.

1 Correct this spelling of CHAUVANISM.
2 A CHARLATAN is a . . . who . . . claims to have . . . or . . .
3 What ingredients would you use to make CHARLOTTE?
4 What is a CHASER?
5 A CHATTEL is an . . . of . . . property.
6 What would happen if your father were to CHASTISE you?
7 Name someone you know or have heard about who has CHARISMA.
8 What are the two plurals of CHATEAU?
9 Name someone you know who is CHARY.
10 Here are five words. Write a sentence for each one to show you know its meaning.

chasm checkers chat up
chauffeur chassis

11 Write two sentences for each of these words to show two of their meanings.

charm chase check cheat
charter

12 The letters 'che' appear at the top right-hand side of the page. Why are they there?
13 Look at the entry for the word CHARM[1].
(a) What does the *n* stand for?
(b) Write sentences to show you know how to use the word *in three different ways*.
14 Look at the entry for the word CHEAP[2].
(a) What do *adj* and *adv* stand for?
(b) Write sentences to show you know how to use the word *in four different ways*.

Talking and listening

15 Form groups of five or six.
See that you have a dictionary each.

Take turns to call a word from anywhere in the dictionary.
When the word is called open your dictionaries to where you think the word should be.
Pages must not be turned once the dictionary is open.
The person getting the page nearest to the word wins the round.
The game is won by the first person to score ten.

Language—punctuation

Punctuation is the use of signs in writing to make the meaning clear.

The sign used more than any other is the full stop. One of the uses of this dot on a line of writing is to end a sentence. It separates a sentence from those around it.

A sentence is a group of words that make complete sense. No one would understand you if you wrote:

Neil Armstrong was the first

but your meaning would be quite clear if you wrote:

Neil Armstrong was the first man to walk on the moon.

Like all sentences this one starts with a capital letter and ends with a full stop. It contains one complete thought.

16 Here are ten unfinished sentences. Complete them so that they make sense. Begin each sentence with a capital letter and end it with a full stop.

She paused before . . .
The wintry sun . . .
After his illness . . .
. . . through the forest
. . . displayed in the window
. . . teeth shaped like a chisel
We halted at . . .
The workmen are . . .
. . . in the spring
. . . the museum this morning

17 There are three sentences in this passage. Write it out putting in the full stops and capital letters.

clothes for the family were made at home wool from their own sheep was spun into thread and woven into cloth by the women skins were tanned for shoes and for harness and for clothes for the men

18 There are five sentences in this passage. Write it out putting in full stops and capital letters.

the gold seekers rushed inland from San Francisco to the rivers and mountain sides where gold had been found there they staked out their claims and started digging gravel and washing it for gold life at the diggings was rough a man who tried to take another's claim was tried by a court of miners and punished men who stole gold were hanged

19 There are five sentences in the following paragraph but they are not in their correct order. Write out the paragraph so that it makes sense.

Almost every family had a garden and grew many of the same vegetables we eat today. The colonists pickled and dried vegetables and kept fruits in covered stone jars for use in winter. In the seventeenth century food in New England was good, and there was plenty of it. Of course there were no refrigerators and foods could not be canned as they are now. Families obtained their meat from cattle, pigs and fowl raised at home, and the supply was increased by wild game which the men and boys shot in the forest.

Writing

20 Here is a paragraph of six sentences that gives information about an egg.

An egg is hen-fresh when it is still warm, and if you boil it then or within 24 hours the white will stay milky. After two days it will set. When the egg is three days old you can make a meringue and at seven days you can really hard boil it. It can still claim to be fresh after a fortnight if it has been kept cool in the dark. Even after that, when it has ceased to taste good, it will still not be bad. How long it has to be kept before it is fit to throw out I do not know.

Write three similar paragraphs giving information about three different things.

21 Write two paragraphs of six sentences each giving information about the following objects in your classroom.
(a) the chairs
(b) the windows

22 Write a paragraph of six sentences about information. What exactly is information? Where do you find it? How do you get it?

Learning at home

23 There are many kinds of dictionary. Here are some of them.

A Dictionary of Quotations and Proverbs
The Dictionary of Phrase and Fable
A Dictionary of Abbreviations
A Dictionary of Music
A Dictionary of Geology

Make a list of the dictionaries in your school and public libraries. For each one give the full title and the publisher.

24 The letters 'che' at the top right of the extract on page 4 are known as *guide letters*. They are there to help you find a word quickly. Some dictionaries use *guide words* instead of letters.
The letters 'che' show that words beginning with those letters are at the bottom of that page.
Use any dictionary to find and write down ten words that come between these guide words:

cotton duel

25 From questions 13 and 14 you will have seen that each word in a dictionary is called an *entry*. Use any dictionary to look up the entries for each of the following.

helot lemur skewbald papoose

Note and write out the information each entry gives.

Maps and Pictures

Sometimes maps and pictures give more information than words.

You will be using both in other subjects taken at school so it is important to know how to get information from them.

On page 8 there is a map of the Croyde Bay area of Devon. At the bottom of that map is a line marked off into pieces or segments. The line is called a *scale of miles* and is used to measure distances on the map. On this scale one segment equals one quarter ($\frac{1}{4}$) of a mile.

To use the scale follow these steps:

- Lay a sheet of paper on the map with its edge as a straight line from the Scenic Viewpoint (see ⛯ Legend) at Coastguard Lookout to the Scenic Viewpoint between Ramson Cliff and Napp's Cliff. All these can be found at the top of the map.
- Put two pencil marks on the edge of the paper, one for each viewpoint.
- Place the edge of your marked paper just below the scale of miles. Match the mark for the Coastguard Lookout with the 0 (zero) of the scale.
- Read off on the right of the scale the mark for the other scenic viewpoint. You should find that it is a walking distance of just over one mile along the coastal footpath.

Use this skill to answer questions 1–3 below.

Questions to answer

1 Which is wider Saunton Sand or Croyde Sand?

2 You are staying at Baggy Point Hotel (see ⋆Legend) and would like to walk to Baggy Point and back before breakfast. How far is it there and back?

3 How far is Woodstock Guest House

(see ♠ Legend) from Pencil Rock if you walk across country? You will find that your pencil mark on the right will be off the scale. Simply mark on your paper where the mile comes and then move this mark to the 0 of the scale. Add the extra distance to the mile.

Croyde Bay, Dorset

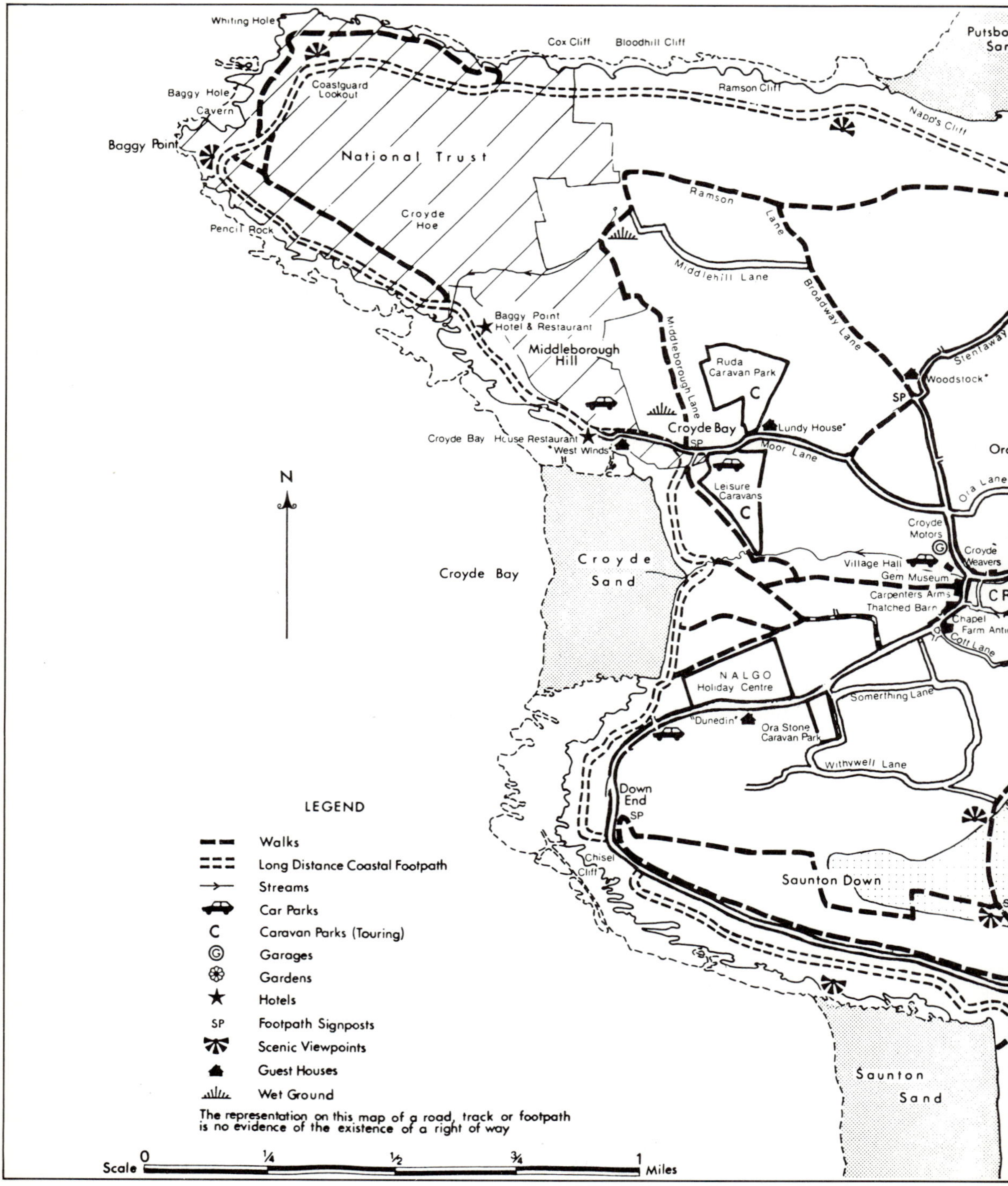

4 Is it possible to walk along the coastal footpath from Down End to Baggy Point?
5 Name the guest house opposite the NALGO Holiday Centre.
6 Is there a car park at Croyde Bay village?
7 Name the guest house south of the Middleborough Hill car park.
8 How many caravan parks are there in Croyde Bay village?
9 Near which lane are there two areas of wet ground?
10 Why is a footpath signpost needed at Down End?
11 Which would be the nearest guest house to stay at if you wanted to explore Saunton Down?

Language

The full stop is also used after an abbreviation. An abbreviation is a shortened word, e.g. P.C. for Police Constable.

12 These abbreviations often appear in newspapers. What countries or organisations do they stand for?

E.E.C.	U.S.S.R.	O.P.E.C.
U.K.	C.A.P.	N.Z.
N.A.T.O.	N.S.W.	U.N.O.

13 Write these abbreviations out in full:

C.I.A.	Q.C.	C.I.D.
S.R.N.	B.T.U.	F.R.G.S.
A.A.A.	B.M.A.	R.N.L.I.

14 These abbreviations are used in a sport. What is the sport and what do the abbreviations mean?

b. st. l.b.w. n.b. n.o.
c. & b.

15 People work for each of the following organisations. What are the organisations and what kind of work might people do?

I.C.I.	B.P.	B.R.S.
I.B.A.	D.H.S.S.	N.A.S.A.

Writing

16 Write the newspaper story that could appear under this headline:

THRILLING RESCUE AT BAGGY POINT

17 Imagine it is early morning and you are standing on Saunton Down facing north. Write two paragraphs describing the view. Start with:

As the morning mist cleared, a splendid scene revealed itself.

18 Write an adventure story that takes place in the Croyde Bay area. You may set it in the past, the present or the future.
19 Imagine the village shopkeeper at Down End is old, short-sighted and very deaf. Write about him, his store and a morning in his shop. Get some of your ideas from the map.
20 Write the diary of an imaginary holiday at Croyde Bay.

Talking and listening

21 You will need to form pairs for these conversations between two people.
No. 1 opens the conversation and No. 2 must agree with what is said. For example:

No. 1 Have you ever been to Croyde Bay?
No. 2 Yes.
No. 1 When?
No. 2 Last year.
No. 1 What was it like?

Continue the conversation with both of you using your imagination.
Start a new conversation when this one is finished.
No. 1 now becomes No. 2.
New opening line:

No. 1 I hear you found a hoard of gold coins on Croyde Hoe.
No. 2 Yes. It was last Saturday morning.

Continue until conversation is finished.
Find someone else to work with.
Decide who is to be No. 1.
Opening line:

No. 1 Excuse me, but aren't you Boy George?
No. 2 Yeah.
No. 1 What are you doing on holiday at Ruda Caravan Park?

22 Form groups of five or six.
Choose a chairperson.
Imagine you are a committee of the Croyde Bay District Council and you have been given £1,000,000 pounds to improve the area. How would you spend the money?
Use the map during your discussion.
Make a brief written report of what you propose.

Learning at home

23 Choose a picture from a colour supplement or a magazine. Tell in about 200 words the information contained in that picture.

Figures and Diagrams

Look carefully at the weather forecast on page 11.

Questions to answer

Weather—6 a.m. to midnight

1 What maximum temperature centigrade was expected in SW England?
2 What kind of wind was expected in Shetland?
3 From which direction would the wind be blowing in the Channel Islands?
4 Would Edinburgh have any rain?
5 Was sun expected in the Lake District?

Sea Passages

6 What would the sea be like in St George's Channel on that day?
7 Was visibility expected to be good in the English Channel?

Around Britain

8 Would rain be expected in Hastings in the morning or the afternoon?
9 Which town would have the most hours of sunshine?
10 Tell in your own words the weather picture for the day in Manchester.
11 What maximum temperature centigrade was expected in Cromer?
12 Would there be any reason for flights to be cancelled at Birmingham (B'ham) Airport because of weather?

High tides

13 At what time did Swansea expect its morning high tide?
14 When would Dover have its afternoon high tide?
15 Was the expected morning high tide going to be higher at Southampton than Liverpool?

Can you find these?

16 Where in Britain was the highest day temperature on the previous day?
17 At what time did the sun set on that day?
18 Was there rain in the Irish Sea between 6 a.m. and midnight?
19 What was the minimum temperature in London *on the previous day*?
20 When was lighting-up time in Penzance?

Writing

21 Write a five sentence paragraph that starts with:

It was a cold, cold morning.

22 What kind of weather do you like best and why?
23 Write a short story about a storm near your home.
24 Why bother with weather forecasting? To whom does it matter and why? Explain in a page of writing.
25 Describe a very wet day at school.

Weather

A ridge of high pressure covers many areas, frontal troughs will approach the SW later.

6 am to midnight

London, East Anglia, E Midlands, E, NW, SE, central N England: Mostly dry with sunny periods; Wind W light; Max temp 23C (73F).

W Midlands, central S England, N Wales, Channel Islands: Mostly dry with sunny periods; cloudier later with rain during evening; wind SW light to moderate; max temp 22C (72F).

SW England, S Wales: Becoming cloudy with outbreaks of rain; wind SW moderate backing S fresh; max temp 22C (72F).

Lake District, Glasgow, SW Scotland, Northern Ireland, Isle of Man: Dry, sunny periods; wind variable mostly W light; max temp 20C (68F).

Borders, Edinburgh, Dundee, Central Highlands, NE England: Sunny periods, perhaps isolated showers; wind W light; max temp 21C (70F).

Aberdeen, Moray Firth, Argyl, NE, NW Scotland, Orkney: Sunny intervals, scattered showers; wind NW light; max temp 19C (66F).

Shetland: Occasional showers; wind NW moderate; max temp 15C (59F).

Outlook for tomorrow and Friday: Rain spreading to many areas; followed in the W by brighter more showery weather later; temperatures generally near normal; a little above in the E at first and a little below in the W later.

SEA PASSAGES: North Sea, English Channel (E), Strait of Dover: wind W backing SW moderate or fresh, mainly fair; visibility good; sea slight or moderate. St George's Channel, Irish Sea: wind SW moderate backing S fresh or strong; rain later; visibility good becoming moderate; sea slight becoming moderate or rough.

Sun rises:	Sun sets:
5.24 am	8.48 pm
Moon rises:	Moon sets:
10.26 am	11.00 pm

First Quarter: August 4.

Lighting-up time

London 9.18 pm to 4.56 am
Bristol 9.28 pm to 5.06 am
Edinburgh 9.50 pm to 4.49 am
Manchester 9.35 pm to 4.56 am
Penzance 9.35 pm to 5.23 am

Yesterday

Temperatures at midday yesterday: c, cloud; f, fair; r, rain; s, sun.

		C	F			C	F
Belfast	c	17	63	Guernsey	s	19	66
Birmingham	f	21	70	Inverness	r	15	59
Blackpool	f	17	63	Jersey	s	19	66
Bristol	f	19	66	London	c	20	68
Cardiff	f	19	66	Manchester	f	17	63
Edinburgh	r	15	59	Newcastle	c	16	61
Glasgow	c	15	59	Ronaldsway	f	17	63

London

Yesterday: Temp: max 6 am to 6 pm, 24C (75F); min 6 pm to 6 am, 18C (64F). Humidity: 6 pm, 40 per cent. Rain 24hr to 6 pm, 0.02in. Sun: 24 hr to 6 pm, 4.3hr. Bar, mean sea level: 6 pm, 1 012.0 millibars, rising.
1,000 millibars = 29.53in.

Highest and lowest

Yesterday: Highest day temp: Heathrow 25C (77F) lowest day max: Cape Wrath, 13C (55F) highest rainfall: Carlisle, 0.97in. highest sunshine: Tenby 10.8hr

NOON TODAY Pressure is shown in millibars FRONTS Warm Cold Occluded (Symbols are on advancing edge)

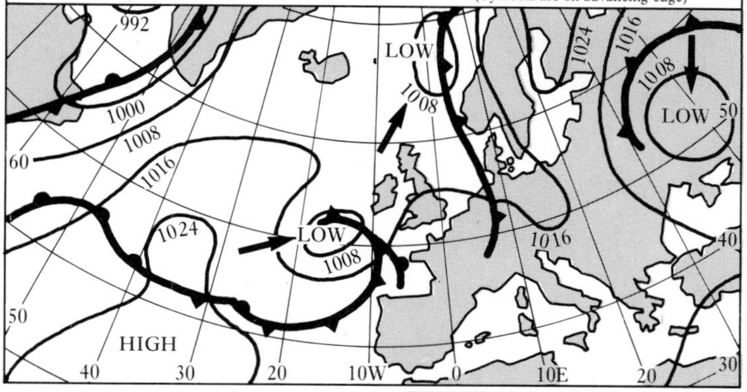

NOON TODAY

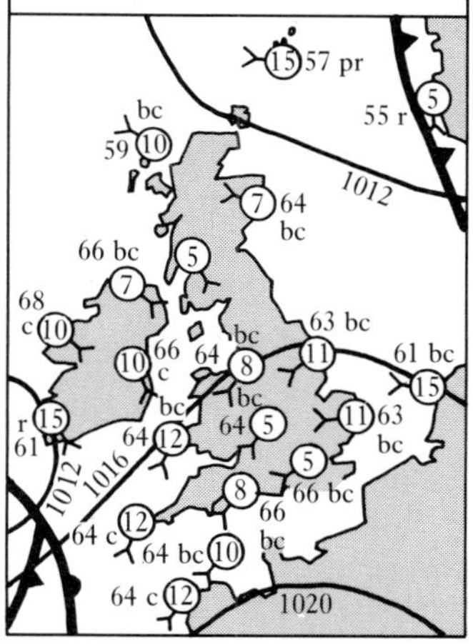

b-blue sky; bc-blue sky and cloud; c-cloudy; o-overcast; f-fog; d-drizzle; h-hail; m-mist; r-rain; s-snow; th-thunderstorm; p-showers. Arrows show wind direction, wind speed (mph) circled. Temperatures fahrenheit.

High Tides

TODAY

	AM	HT	PM	HT
London Bridge	5.26	7.4	5.40	7.2
Aberdeen	4.38	4.5	5.23	4.2
Avonmouth	11.00	13.4	11.17	13.5
Belfast	2.19	3.9	2.52	3.4
Cardiff	10.45	12.3	11.02	12.4
Devonport	9.48	5.3	10.01	5.6
Dover	2.26	6.6	2.49	6.7
Falmouth	9.18	5.1	9.31	5.4
Glasgow	4.14	5.0	4.56	4.5
Harwich	3.24	4.1	3.42	3.9
Holyhead	1.35	5.8	2.06	5.4
Hull	9.43	7.7	10.22	7.4
Ilfracombe	9.44	9.1	10.04	9.3
Leith	6.05	5.6	6.38	5.5
Liverpool	2.37	9.7	3.04	9.3
Lowestoft	1.04	2.5	1.01	2.6
Margate	3.39	4.8	3.47	4.8
Milford Haven	9.57	6.9	10.17	7.1
Newquay	8.49	6.9	9.10	7.1
Oban	9.27	3.7	9.32	4.0
Penzance	8.54	5.4	9.06	5.7
Portland	10.57	2.0	10.58	2.2
Portsmouth	2.44	4.7	3.26	4.8
Shoreham	2.41	6.3	3.14	6.4
Southampton	2.06	4.5	2.43	4.6
Swansea	10.01	9.3	10.21	9.4
Tees	7.07	5.6	7.46	5.3
Walton-on-Naze	3.13	4.4	3.27	4.3

Tide measurement in metres: 1m-3.2808ft.

Around Britain

	Sun hr	Rain in	Max C	Max F	
Scarboro	4.6	—	21	70	Sunny pm
Bridlington	4.0	—	22	72	Cloudy
Cromer	2.9	—	23	73	Bright
Lowestoft	1.9	.06	23	73	Shwrs pm
Clacton	1.1	.01	22	72	Cloudy
Margate	0.5	.04	22	72	Rain pm
Folkestone	1.6	.04	19	66	Shwrs am
Hastings	2.2	.06	20	68	Rain am
Eastbourne	2.2	.03	19	66	Rain am
Brighton	—	—	19	66	Sunny pm
Worthing	4.2	—	20	68	Bright pm
Littlehamptn	5.9	.02	21	70	Sunny pm
Bognor R	7.0	.05	21	70	Sunny pm
Southsea	6.3	.02	23	73	Sunny
Shanklin	7.5	.03	21	70	Sunny pm
Bournemth	5.5	.06	22	72	Sunny pm
Poole	5.0	.20	22	72	Cloudy
Swanage	7.3	.14	21	70	Sunny
Weymouth	6.9	.21	20	68	Bright
Exmouth	—	—	—	—	—
Torquay	6.3	.05	23	73	Shwrs pm
Falmouth	9.0	.06	20	68	Shwrs pm
Penzance	9.4	.10	21	70	Sunny

	Sun hr	Rain in	Max C	Max F	
Guernsey	9.8	.24	21	70	Sunny
Scilly Isles	10.5	—	20	68	Sunny
Newquay	8.3	.12	23	73	Bright
Ilfracombe	8.7	.08	20	68	Sunny
Tenby	10.8	.26	20	68	Sunny
Southport	6.0	.22	19	66	Sunny pm
Morecambe	4.9	.44	18	64	Sunny pm
Douglas	8.6	.37	18	64	Sunny pm
London (Ctrl)	4.3	.01	24	75	Bright
B'ham (Airpt)	6.7	.09	23	73	Sunny
Bristol (Ctrl)	8.1	.17	21	70	Sunny pm
Cardiff (Ctrl)	9.4	.25	20	68	Sunny
Anglesey	6.3	.93	18	64	Rain am
B'pool (Airpt)	5.4	.30	18	64	Shwrs am
Manchester	1.8	.19	19	66	Rain am
Nottingham	6.1	.24	21	70	Shwrs
N'ctl-n-Tyne	1.5	.22	19	66	Shwrs
Carlisle	2.8	.97	18	64	Rain am
Eskdalemuir	0.7	.52	16	61	Rain
Prestwick	3.7	.20	18	64	Rain am
Glasgow	1.0	.16	18	64	Bright pm
Tiree	8.1	.07	17	63	Sunny
Stornoway	1.5	.03	17	63	Cloudy

Language—nouns and adjectives

> EDINBURGH, ABERDEEN, CENTRAL HIGHLANDS
> *Showers* or longer outbreaks of *rain* with some sunny *intervals; temperatures* near normal; night *fog* patches developing.

All the words in italics are COMMON NOUNS. These name things and creatures, e.g. snow, ice, sleet, bear, skier, toboggan.
The words in capital letters are PROPER NOUNS.
These are the names of persons and places and begin with a capital letter, e.g. Paris, Peter, Ark Royal, Robin Hood, Pacific Ocean, Hong Kong.

26 Look under 'SEA PASSAGES' on page 11. Make a list of all Common and Proper nouns under that heading.

27 Copy out this passage and fill in each blank with a noun.

Light . . . was falling in many . . . of the . . . tonight when great . . . of holiday-makers made for . . . after one of the sunniest Easters for many . . .. During the last few hours . . . and coaches from . . . and country have been packed with returning . . .. On the . . . it has been one of the quietest . . . Holidays ever known, with cars numbered in . . . instead of the usual thousands. An Automobile . . . count this morning on the . . . to Brighton road totalled thirty . . . in two hours, compared with three thousand an . . . in bad . . . last year.

28 It's a *warm* wind, the *west* wind, full of birds' cries;
I never hear the *west* wind but tears are in my eyes;
For it comes from the *west* lands, the old *brown* hills,
And April's in the *west* wind, and daffodils.

This is the poet John Masefield describing a wind. The words in italics are ADJECTIVES.
Adjectives help to tell more about nouns. We use adjectives to describe animals, places, things and people.
Masefield uses the adjectives in italics to describe the kind of wind, the kind of cries, the kind of lands and the kind of hills.

29 List all the adjectives in this passage. Remember that adjectives tell more about nouns.
Ask your teacher if you are not sure about a word being used as an adjective.

Although the sun shone brightly, the morning was cold. Later the wind rose, and the cold became bitter and piercing. Low heavy clouds appeared, trailing showers across the plain below us. With each freshening gust of wind, dust curtains whirled up from the bare red patches. They mingled with the low-hanging clouds, making it impossible to tell whether the haze advancing on us was wet or dry.

Talking and listening

30 Form groups of five.
Choose a chairperson who will need a watch with a second hand.
Each of the remaining four must speak for one minute without hesitation or repetition on one of the topics below.
Six points are won if this is done.
Penalty points are deducted one at a time for hesitation and repetition.
Repeat until each member of the group has acted as chairperson.
These topics must not be repeated.

boys	parents
thunderstorms	cars
accidents	unemployment
truth	rules
policemen	fox-hunting
rhubarb	ambulances
aircraft	holidays
fashions	dogs

trains	pets
sleep	television
friendship	showers
food	girls
enemies	dentists
smoking	bullying

31 Form groups of five or six.
Discuss and plan a short programme for radio about a hurricane that sweeps through the West Indies.
Choose between a play and a talk with interviews.
If it is a play then make sure the conversation is written down like that on page 9.
Tape record the programme for playback to other groups.
It is your responsibility as a group to find a tape recorder.

Learning at home

32 Go through the alphabet and write down the name of (a) an animal, and (b) a flower that begins with each letter. Use the library to help you.

33 On a map of Europe find and write down:
(a) two countries whose names begin with P
(b) three countries whose names begin with S
(c) six capital cities whose names begin with B
(d) five rivers
(e) four mountains
(f) four lakes

Information for Parliament

When Parliament needs information it sometimes sets up a Royal Commission to find out what is happening.

On page 14 is part of the *Report of the Royal Commission into the Mines, 1842.*

Down the mine father hewed the coal. Mother, as drawer, had a belt round her waist and went on all fours pulling a truck. Sometimes she stood waist-deep in water, her clothes wet all day, her skin raw with the friction of the chain.

The children carried the coal up ladders in baskets of half-a-hundred-weight at a time, their bodies bent and, when the baskets were full, with lumps of coal placed on their necks. Smaller children pushed small trucks along the passages which were so low that even the smallest had to stoop. Children had to work the pumps, the cages and the doors which conducted the air up the shafts—a three-year-old being quite capable of managing this last not very arduous labour, though it involved twelve hours sitting alone and mostly in the dark, opening and closing the doors.

Questions to answer

1 Which member of the family cut the coal?
2 In one sentence, explain the position mother had to adopt in order to pull a truck.
3 What were the other working conditions like for mother?
4 How was extra coal carried by the children when their baskets were full?
5 Name four jobs done by children in the mines in 1842.
6 What do the following words mean? Use a dictionary if you wish.

hewed friction stoop shafts arduous

7 Give the passage a title.

Writing

8 Write a report about any family work situation. Follow the pattern of the passage above. For example, you might start:

In the bedroom father was painting the doors . . . .

9 In six sentences write about the working conditions of the children on page 13.
10 Write five sentences that give information about Robin Hood. The first is done for you:

Robin Hood was an outlaw.

11 Write a page of information about Hallowe'en.

Understanding

12 Here are two passages each with twenty words left out.
The first gives information about the cotton plant and the second about animals in Australia.
Each blank is numbered. Write down that number and put the missing word beside it. You may find there is more than one word that fits, but only one is needed.

(a) The cotton plant is (1) . . . of the miracles of (2) . . .. It grows in warm (3) . . . lands where the climate (4) . . . soil are suitable. Each (5) . . . grows to between four (6) . . . six feet and produces (7) . . . twenty lovely flowers which (8) . . . for only three days. (9) . . . the petals drop off (10) . . . small green pods remain. (11) . . . contain the new seeds, (12) . . . forty of them in (13) . . . pod, and every one is (14) . . . to soft downy hairs (15) . . . those of dandelion clocks. (16) . . . pods keep swelling for (17) . . . two months until they (18) . . . about as big as (19) . . . eggs before bursting open (20) . . . reveal the cotton.

(b) The animals of Australia (1) . . . even more peculiar than (2) . . . trees. Australia is the chief (3) . . . of the marsupials, animals (4) . . . as kangaroos, which (5) . . . their young in the (6) . . . pouch. The only large native (7) . . . which is not a (8) . . . is the dingo or (9) . . . dog. Although kangaroos are still (10) . . . enough in the less-settled (11) . . ., most Australian children are (12) . . . likely to have seen (13) . . ., and their small cousins (14) . . . wallabies, in a zoo (15) . . . in the bush. The (16) . . ., teddy-bear-like koala is (17) . . . seen mostly in (18) . . . or animal sanctuaries. Wombats, (19) . . . huge guinea-pigs, and woolly-coated possums (20) . . . the most common native animals in the more settled regions.

Language—verbs

The report on page 14 tells us how families worked in the mines in the last century.
In it we learn that:

father *hews* the coal
mother *pulls* the trucks
children *carry* the coal

All those words in *italics* are actions. Words used to describe actions are called VERBS.

13 Can you list all the verbs in this passage? Ask if you are not sure.

An iron mine is very much like a coal mine, but the ore is harder and more difficult to get out. The iron ore has to be melted to extract the iron. This process requires great heat. To make a fire hot enough to smelt the iron from the ore, coke is mixed with the ore and is ignited, and then a strong blast of hot air is blown through the burning mixture. Coke is used for fuel, and limestone is added to help in separating the iron from the ore. Smelting is carried out in a tall tower which is known as a blast furnace.

Talking and listening

14 Form groups of four.
Choose one person to make up the beginning of a story.
Each member of the group then continues the story for as long as possible.

15 Form groups of five.
Each member of the group chooses to be someone in the news but doesn't tell the others.
Questions are then asked by the remainder to find out who the personality can be.

Learning at home

ADVERBS describe or tell us more about verbs. They say in a single word how, where or when the action in a verb takes place. In the sentence *He drove dangerously down the hill* it is the word *dangerously* which tells *how* he drove. Dangerously is therefore an adverb.

All adverbs which say *how* an action is done are known as adverbs of *Manner*.

16 Write six sentences using ONE of the following adverbs of manner in each:

eagerly	secretly	immediately
truthfully	carefully	beautifully

17 Write down three adverbs that go well with each of the following verbs:

to walk	to speak	to smile
to work	to pull	to arrive

All adverbs which say *where* an action takes place are adverbs of *Place*.

18 Write six sentences using ONE of the following adverbs of place in each:

everywhere	hither	nowhere
here	out	anywhere

All adverbs which say *when* an action takes place are adverbs of *Time*.

19 Write six sentences using ONE of the following adverbs of time in each:

daily	yesterday	meanwhile
then	lately	never

2 Description

Language for description can be thought of as a photograph that shows what a person, place or thing looks like. It is the 'world' in which a story moves.

Good, clear description comes from watching closely and accurately. This can be seen in all the following passages whether they are descriptions of people, places or things.

Contents

People

A tall man stood in the doorway. He held a crushed Stetson hat under his arm while he combed his long, black, damp hair straight back. Like the others, he wore blue jeans and a short denim jacket. When he had finished combing his hair he moved into the room, and he moved with a majesty only achieved by royalty and master craftsmen. He was a jerkline skinner, the prince of the ranch, capable of driving ten, sixteen, even twenty mules with a single line to the leaders. He was capable of killing a fly on the wheeler's butt with a bull whip without touching the mule. There was a gravity in his manner and a quiet so profound that all talk stopped when he spoke. His authority was so great that his word was taken on any subject, be it politics or love. This was Slim, the jerkline skinner. His hatchet face was ageless. He might have been thirty-five or fifty. His ear heard more than was said to him, and his slow speech had overtones not of thought, but of understanding beyond thought. His hands, large and lean, were as delicate in their action as those of a temple dancer.

John Steinbeck
Of Mice and Men

An old woman was seated in a decrepit armchair beside the fire. Her small, stringy hands, with the fingers bent and roughened by time, disease and work, were empty in her lap. Empty, too, were her dim eyes and the soft, almost senile features. Only the lines of age showed on the pale flesh. She was dressed in an old black skirt and faded blouse over which she was wearing a red cardigan which was darned coarsely in several places with badly matched wool. Around her body was a heavy black shawl whose folds swathed her shoulders and arms, and which had evidently fallen from her head, which it had recently covered, for the grey hair was disordered in untidy strands, and the little comb at the back of her head was hanging loosely.

F L Green
Odd Man Out

Questions to answer

'A tall man . . .'

1 What kind of hair did Slim have? Was he proud of his hair? Give a reason for your answer.
2 What kind of a face is a 'hatchet' face?
3 Tell in your own words how Slim moved.
4 Give an example of his skill as a jerkline skinner.
5 What was Slim's speech like? Tell in your own words.
6 In a cowboy film would Slim be a 'goodie' or a 'baddie'? Give your reasons.
7 Write out the simile (see page 119) in the last sentence. Is this a good or a bad description? Say why.

'An old woman . . .'

8 Use a dictionary to write out the meaning of the following words.

decrepit senile swathed strands

9 What caused the old woman's hands to be bent and roughened?
10 The hands are described as being 'stringy'. Say whether or not you think this is a good description of an old person's hands. Give your reasons.
11 How does the writer use the old woman's clothing to show her lack of money?
12 Why do you think the dim eyes were 'empty'?
13 How came the grey hair to be 'disordered in untidy strands'?
14 How do we know that the old woman was not able to take care of herself properly?

Writing

We learnt on pages 12 and 15 that adjectives and adverbs play an important part in description.

Remember to use them with care when you attempt the following.

15 Stroke your hair several times. What does it feel like? Write down a few adjectives to describe that feeling.
16 What does your hand feel like? Describe this feeling in a sentence or two.
17 Write down some adjectives to describe the feeling of walking barefoot on a pebbly beach.
18 Describe the sensation of ice cream in your mouth.
19 How would you describe anger? Try to remember the last time you were angry.
20 Write a description of yourself.
Tell what you look like, what sort of boy or girl you are, and what it feels like to be you.
Try to put down both good and bad points.

21 Think of some relations or friends who live in another town.
First, describe who they are and what they look like, then go on to describe the home.
Finally, describe the district in which they live.

22 Describe the most pleasant or the most amusing person you have ever met.

23 Imagine you are a detective working in a large supermarket and you suspect a man and a woman of shoplifting.
Write a good description of the two people so that other staff in the store can recognise them.
Include the following in your description:

height, build, apparent age, clothing, shoes, colour of complexion, eyes and hair and any peculiarities of walk, speech and manner.

Language—the comma

The comma (,) is the shortest pause in a sentence. It is used to:

indicate a short pause in reading

e.g. When he saw the strange light in the sky above him, he was afraid.

separate strings of nouns, verbs, adjectives and adverbs

e.g. Fiona bought almonds, sultanas, herbs, lemon juice, sugar and eggs.
The burglar entered the room slowly, silently, carefully and furtively.

give the right meaning

e.g. Mary, my sister, is staying in tonight.
Mary, my sister is staying in tonight.

separate a sequence of actions or instructions

e.g. Heat the oil in a frying pan, add the sandwich rounds, fry until golden brown on both sides, drain on absorbent paper, garnish and serve.

mark off a phrase in a sentence

e.g. If you walk under a ladder, some people say, you will have bad luck.

mark off a word or words that begin a sentence

e.g. By the way, I shall not be coming with you tomorrow. Nevertheless, the homework will be done.

divide numbers

e.g. 61,486,876
614,868
6,148

Use the information above to help you put commas in the following.

24 (a) Breathless he could run no more.
(b) Yes I will be at school tomorrow.
(c) Ladies and gentlemen I will be as brief as I can.
(d) There are 55671863 people in Great Britain and Northern Ireland.
(e) Five gold rings four calling birds three french hens two turtle doves and a partridge in a pear tree.
(f) First I would like to know where you were yesterday.
(g) The strikers who were breaking the windows were arrested by the police.
(h) Verity Mealing my best friend is coming shopping with me.
(i) Melt the fat in the frying pan soften the spring onions in the hot fat add the beans corn and parsley cook until the vegetables are heated through.
(j) The woman was old toothless wrinkled dirty and thoroughly objectionable.

Listening

Ask your teacher to give the following listening tests.

25 Write and punctuate a dictation passage of about 150 words. Correct spelling will be required.

26 Listen to a comprehension passage of up to 400 words on which you will be asked five questions. Use the following test procedure:

- The five questions should be in front of you.

- The passage is to be read twice at normal speed.
- During the first reading do not look at the questions or write anything.
- Look at the questions when the first reading is finished.
- Wait one minute before the second reading.
- Look at the questions during the second reading.
- Write answers to the five questions.

Learning at home

27 Choose from any newspaper, magazine or book a passage of about 200 words. Tell, *in about 60 of your own words*, what this passage is about.
If you have difficulty, ask an older person in the house for help.

Describing people

Ledyard was a small, thin-featured man, a pedlar or trader who came through every couple of months with things you would not get at the general store in town. He would pack his stock in a mule-team freighter driven by an old, white-haired Negro who acted like he was afraid even to speak without permission. Ledyard would make deliveries in his buckboard, driving a hard bargain always and picking up orders for articles to bring on the next trip. I did not like him, and not just because he said nice things about me he did not mean for my father's benefit. He smiled too much and there was no friendliness in it.

Jack Schaefer
Shane

Oh! but he was a tight-fisted hand at the grindstone. Scrooge! a squeezing, wrenching, grasping, scraping, clutching, covetous old sinner! Hard and sharp as a flint, from which no steel had ever struck out generous fire; secret and self-contained and solitary as an oyster. The cold within him froze his old features, nipped his pointed nose, shrivelled his cheek, stiffened his gait; made his eyes red, his thin lips blue; and spoke out shrewdly in his grating voice. A frosty rime was on his head, and on his eyebrows, and on his wiry chin. He carried his own low temperature always about with him; he iced his office in the dog-days; and didn't thaw it one degree at Christmas.

Charles Dickens
A Christmas Carol

Questions to answer

Ledyard

1 Where might this have taken place? Give your reasons.
2 What is meant by 'things'? (line 8)
3 Why did Ledyard use an old, white-haired Negro to drive his mule-team freighter?
4 'Like he was afraid' (lines 4–5) is not very good English. Write it out a better way.

5 What is a 'buckboard'? (line 6)
6 What was the storyteller's main reason for disliking Ledyard?
7 Tell of Ledyard's bad qualities in your own words.

Scrooge

8 Use a dictionary to write out the meaning of the following:

covetous shrivelled gait rime wiry dog-days

9 List seven adjectives in the passage that show Scrooge to be a mean person.
10 Write out the simile (see page 119) in the passage that tells us Scrooge lived alone and kept himself to himself.
11 How does the description of the face of Scrooge show his cold nature?
12 Explain in your own words 'he iced his office in the dog-days'.
13 What was it on the head, eyebrows and chin of Scrooge that looked like 'frosty rime'?
14 Tell in your own words how the mean and cold nature of Scrooge is brought out in the description.

Writing

15 Think of a friend or relative.
Write a detailed description of that person's clothes and jewellery.
16 Describe the possessions of any adult you know. What do they say about that person?
17 Think of an adult you find difficult to understand. Try to describe him or her.
18 Describe a time when you were very happy and what it felt like.
19 Write a description of the faces in the photographs on pages 18, 19 and here.
20 Look through your English exercise book. Mark any description you have made of a person. Take any two and try to improve those descriptions.
21 Read with care the poems on pages 117 and 128 about people (The Knifesmith and Mr Kartoffel). Try writing your own poem about a person you know.

Edward III

Eleanor of Castile

Language—the exclamation mark

Oh! but he was a tight-fisted hand at the grindstone.

The punctuation mark (!) is called an exclamation mark. An exclamation (or a crying out) is a word or words showing a sudden strong feeling.
e.g. Help!
Fire!
Oh! my arm!
This is the best way to use an exclamation mark in your writing.

There are two other ways. It can be used to:

draw attention to a command
e.g. Quick march!
Go away!
Come back here!

show amusement, disgust or sarcasm
e.g. She was silly enough to turn up at the disco wearing yellow wellies!
What a stupid boy you are!
And you're supposed to be the expert!

Remember also the following:

when it is repeated it must be placed after the last word
e.g. Ha, ha, ha!
and NOT Ha! Ha! Ha!

it contains a full stop but it need not be followed by a capital letter
e.g. Excellent! you have done really well.

in school it should be used one at a time
e.g. It's a goal!
A fat lot of good that will do!
Of course, when writing to a friend you can use as many as you like!
e.g. Was my face red!!!

Use the information above to help you with the following. Pick out the sentences below that need an exclamation mark and write them with that mark in your book.

22 (a) Let me go at once.
(b) A golf course has eighteen holes.
(c) He talks a lot of stupid nonsense.
(d) Cotton is a fibre.
(e) Be quick.
(f) What a fine cook you are.
(g) Have you enjoyed yourselves.
(h) What do you notice about the vowels in the word facetious.
(i) How well you look.
(j) The wind is cold today.

Talking and listening

Form groups of four.

23 Each member of the group chooses a favourite television character.
Discuss the characters chosen.
Write descriptions of the four characters.

24 Talk about the different kinds of teachers you have known.
The *type* of teacher is important and not the name.
Write descriptions of four different types of teacher.

Learning at home

25 Write an accurate description of a neighbour or someone who visits your house each day.

Places

Dark spruce forests frowned on either side of the frozen waterway. The trees had been stripped by a recent wind of their covering of frost. A vast silence reigned over the land.

But there was life abroad in the land. Down the frozen waterways toiled a string of wolfish dogs. Their bristly fur was rimed with frost. Their breath froze in the air as it left their mouths. Leather harness was on the dogs, and leather traces attached them to a sled which dragged along behind. On the sleds were blankets, an axe, a coffee-pot, and a frying pan.

In advance of the dogs, on wide snow-shoes, toiled a man. At the rear of the sled toiled a second man. Their bodies were covered with fur and soft-tanned leather.

Jack London
White Fang

So I took my paddle and slid out from shore just a step or two, and then let the canoe drop along down amongst the shadows. The moon was shining, and outside of the shadows it made it most as light as day. . . . A little ripply, cool breeze begun to blow, and that was as good as saying the night was about done. I give her a turn with the paddle, and brung her nose to shore; then I got my gun and slipped out and into the edge of the wood. I set down there on a log and looked out through the leaves. I see the moon go off watch and the darkness begin to blanket the river. But in a little while I see a pale streak over the tree-tops, and knowed the day was coming. . . . By-and-by . . . I catch a glimpse of fire, away through the trees.

Mark Twain
The Adventures of Huckleberry Finn

Questions to answer

'Dark spruce forests . . .'
This passage describes men moving through a part of Alaska. In the first sentence the words *forests* and *waterway* tell about the kind of scene. How many more words are there like this?

1 Write out all the other words in the passage that give information about the natural scene.

Blankets and *axe* in line 8 tell about man and his way of life in that area.

2 List all the words in the passage that do the same thing.
3 Why were the spruce trees dark and not covered with frost?
4 What was the 'life' which was abroad in the land?
5 Which word tells that it was hard going for the dogs?
6 What are 'traces'?
7 You met the word 'rime' on page 21. What does it mean?
How does its use differ here?
8 How were the men protected against the cold?

'So I took my paddle . . .'
In this paragraph Huck paddles his canoe down the Mississippi River.

His senses (sight, hearing, smell, taste and touch) let him know about the scene around him.

For example, he *saw* that *the moon was shining*.

9 List every time Huck used his senses in the paragraph. Do it like this:

moon sight

10 Why was it not light in Huck's part of the river?
11 What message did the breeze give to Huck?
12 How did Huck bring the canoe to shore?
13 What is meant by 'I see the moon go off watch'?
14 How did Huck know that the day was coming?
15 For what had Huck been waiting whilst sitting on the log?

Writing

16 Imagine yourself lost in a wood in a heavy thunderstorm. Describe what it was like and how, because you had been warned of the danger of sheltering under trees, you attempted to get out of the wood.
17 Here is a sentence-picture of sunrise.
'The sleepy sun rose brooding from the sea, golden and soft, searching far horizons with its hazy shafts of light.'
Write similar sentence-pictures for the following scenes:

the wind on a stormy night
the lights of a fairground
a waterfall in sunshine
smoke rising from a factory chimney

18 Write a story in which you are very small and live in a place you know well. Describe how everything appears to you, and tell how you feel, what you enjoy and what frightens you.

19 Describe one of the following:

a sea front in winter
a foggy night in a city

20 Write a detailed description of a room you know well.

21 Describe your school on (a) a wet and windy day, and (b) a pleasant, warm and sunny day.

22 Write a sentence or two describing each of the following motions:

a car skidding
a water skier swinging out on an arc
a jagged streak of lightning

Language—the hyphen

coffee-pot *snow-shoes* *soft-tanned leather*

The punctuation mark (-) is called a hyphen. The hyphen is used to:

join two or more words to make a single compound word

e.g. by-and-by
detective-inspector
son-in-law
governor-general

join two or more words to make a compound adjective

e.g. soft-tanned leather
red-hot poker
hard-working man
left-handed child

link the words in some place names

e.g. Sonning-on-Thames
Shipston-on-Stour
St Michael's-on-Wyre

avoid giving the wrong impression

e.g. a sweet-shop assistant is not the same as a sweet shop assistant *link prefixes such as 'anti', 'ex' and 'pro' to nouns*

e.g. pre-war
ex-champion
anti-aircraft
pro-British

write spelt-out fractions and numbers between 21 and 99

e.g. one-sixth
three-quarters
four-fifths

e.g. thirty-three
ninety-two
twenty-five

show that a word broken at the end of a line is continued at the beginning of the next line

e.g. I want to ride in tourna-
ments
in towns like Man-
chester
little houses without spaces for gar-
dens

Note that the break in the word should be made to give the reader a clue to the whole word.

e.g. pain-ful and not pai-nful

Use the information above to help you write out and decide whether or not to insert hyphens in each of the following.

23 (a) Everything was looking spick and span.
(b) All the children looked well cared for.
(c) The colour was sea green.
(d) There were fifty six people at the wedding.
(e) An emerald green scarf will not go well with ginger red hair.
(f) He had a rough and ready manner.
(g) The American born bride to be was called Marilyn.
(h) She had a bird like nose.
(i) I missed the two fifteen train.
(j) He was an old age pensioner.
(k) Her father was a pickled onion merchant.
(l) Their holiday was spent in France at Aix les Bains and not at Southend on Sea.
(m) He is an ex champion jockey who rode many winners in the pre war years.

Learning at home

24 Here is a description of a back garden as seen from a window of a house.
Read it carefully and then make a drawing of this garden.

There are trees in tubs on a paved terrace which stands at the top of steps leading down to a path. This path has a lawn on its right and two rockeries on the left. The lawn is surrounded by flower beds. Beyond the lawn are steps leading to a paved sunk garden, with seat and pool, around which there are vegetable and fruit plots. There is a greenhouse to the left, and a tool-shed, herb garden and compost heap, placed behind a trellis across the end of the vegetable, fruit and sunken garden.

Ask for help from an older person in your house if you have difficulty.

Come and Have a Look

Very slowly, while I rocked a sleepy Edward in my arms, she drew out of me the story of my struggle to go to night school, the fact that I had no clothing to speak of and the other children very little. And with a catch of self-pity in my voice, I finished up, 'There doesn't seem to be much hope for anything better for me, unless I can be free to go to work. But there is nobody to look after little Edward, if I do go.'

'But things seem to be getting better,' she comforted me. 'This room is very nicely furnished.'

'I'd rather Edward had some shoes and socks,' I retorted suddenly. 'And you should see the other rooms.'

The dam burst. 'Come and see,' I almost ordered her, and strode to the open door. 'Come and have a look.'

Without a word, her face very serious now, she got up and followed me.

Up the stairs she trudged after me, to the icy, fetid bedrooms, to inspect three iron beds with thin, old-fashioned felt mattresses on them, the urine stains uncovered by any sheet. I had tidied up the bits of blanket and old coats which we used to cover us, and some of the pillows had grubby, white pillow-cases on them.

She looked, aghast, at the door on which I slept. It was balanced on four bricks, one at each corner, and had wads of old newspaper piled on it, instead of a mattress, with a grey piece of sheeting to tuck over them. There was no other furniture, and, of course, there was no bathroom.

In a passion, I swept her downstairs again, to look at the living room, with its bare deal table, assorted straight chairs and upturned paint cans helping out as seats. The only sign of comfort was an old, wooden rocking chair and a very ancient, greasy-looking easy chair, in which was curled a stray cat which Brian had earlier brought in from the rain. On the tiled floor lay a piece of coconut matting, filled with dust. In the old-fashioned iron fireplace I had laid the fire, ready for the children's return home.

The kitchen looked quite large because there was so little in it. A small table flanked the gas stove, and there was a built-in soapstone sink in one corner. The opposite corner was taken up by a brick copper, with a tiny fireplace under it, for boiling washing. Our single bucket stood under the sink; our only wash basin caught the steady drip from the house's cold water tap.

Long lines of shelves ran down one side of the kitchen. They held a motley assortment of rough, white dishes and cups, two saucepans and a dripping tin. A kettle sat on the gas stove beside a tin teapot. A small wooden table held our bits of food, a packet of tea and a blue-bagged pound of sugar, some margarine in a saucer and a new loaf.

I was shivering with cold and with emotion, and my visitor turned pitying, gentle eyes upon me. 'Don't you have a fire?' she asked. They were the first words she had spoken during our lightning tour.

Helen Forrester
Liverpool Miss

Language—quotation marks

'Don't you have a fire?' she asked. (line 46)

The punctuation marks (' ') are called quotation marks. Quotation marks are used to show:

words that are spoken

Such words may come at the beginning of a sentence, e.g.

'You shouldn't make jokes if you can't tell them properly,' said Samantha.

at the end, e.g.

Samantha said, 'You shouldn't make jokes if you can't tell them properly.'

or at both beginning and end, e.g.

'You shouldn't make jokes,' said Samantha, 'if you can't tell them properly.'

NOTICE THAT:

- commas separate the words spoken from the others, e.g.

  Samantha said, 'You shouldn't . . .'

- spoken words begin with capital letters but carry on with small ones, e.g.

  'You shouldn't . . .,' said Samantha, 'if you . . .'

- all other punctuation marks go inside quotation marks, e.g.

  'Don't you have a fire?' she asked.

titles of books, plays, poems, names of aircraft, ships, etc.

e.g. We saw the videotape of 'Animal Farm' in school today.
We have to write about a poem called 'Winter the Huntsman' for homework tonight.
The American airship 'Akron' crashed into the icy waters of the Atlantic on 3 April 1933.

when slang, single words or groups of words are part of a sentence

e.g. Martine's brother is a real 'klutz'.
It is a cowboy saying that you go to the 'land of the setting sun' when you die.
British 'high tea' may be served in the afternoon or early evening.

a quotation that comes inside the words spoken

Double quotation marks (" ") are needed for this.

e.g. She said 'I don't think I'll have time to see "Gregory's Girl" tonight.'
'In class yesterday,' said Gwen, 'I was reading "Private—Keep Out!".'
She then asked, 'Have you read "Z for Zachariah"?'

Use the information above to help you write out and decide where to place quotation and punctuation marks and capital letters in each of the following.

1 (a) the word expert is used so often these days
(b) i cant stand this any longer she shouted
(c) i am never sure how to spell rhododendron
(d) where is my jacket he enquired pathetically
(e) emma replied quietly i think you have made a mistake
(f) the party was organised on a first come first served basis
(g) one more step said slim and ill blow your brains out
(h) shelburn came dancing down the street with an enormous ghettoblaster in his hands
(i) my mother has a copy of macbeth but i am sure she has never read it
(j) its time you were in bed said father
(l) i am surprised said jill i was talking to her just two days ago was she badly hurt
(m) the word before hungry should be felt

Questions to answer

2 Use a dictionary to write out the meaning of the following words.

fetid aghast wads soapstone
motley tour

3 Explain in your own words 'she drew out of me'.

4 The girl telling the story was unable to go to work. Explain why this was so.

5 What were the words of comfort offered by the visitor?

6 What is meant by 'The dam burst'?
7 How did the visitor's manner change when she was ordered to look at the rest of the house?
8 Tell in your own words what the bedrooms were like.
9 What were the only signs of comfort in the living room?
10 Why did the kitchen look so large?
11 How did the visitor's manner change towards the girl after the lightning tour of the house?

Writing

12 These *verbs of saying* can be found in the passage.

she asked   I retorted   I almost ordered

Such verbs of saying show how a speaker is feeling and the tone of voice in which words are spoken.

Write sentences in which you use five other verbs of saying, e.g. *he asked, she whispered*.

13 Imagine you can see in the dark. Write a story showing how you would use this power.
14 Write two interesting descriptions, one of a scene which you think is very ugly, and one of a scene you think very attractive.
15 Write a report for a magazine or newspaper about a serious flood in your area. Describe what happened and the feelings of people involved and made homeless.
16 Describe the view from your bedroom window.
17 A boy or girl is ill in bed.
No one comes to the room for an hour but the patient is not bored. He/she is able to puzzle out what is happening inside and

outside the house by using his/her sense of hearing and of smell.
Imagine you are that patient.
Describe that sixty minutes as vividly as you can.

18 What is it that gives you the creeps or sends shivers up your spine?
Is it spiders, snakes, strange shadows on your bedroom ceiling, or unknown noises outside your window at night?
Describe a particular situation and try to remember your feelings at the time.

Talking and listening

19 Form groups of five, with one member as chairperson.
The chairperson writes in secret any five words on a piece of paper.
The folded paper is then passed to a member of the group.
That person is to tell a story which lasts two or more minutes and brings in the five words.
The other members of the group must listen carefully in order to guess the five words.
Repeat for all the members of the group.

Learning at home

20 Find a magazine or newspaper. Choose an interesting picture that has people in it.
Imagine you are in that picture.
Tell how you feel, what you see, what you smell, what you taste and what you hear.

21 Look through the sports pages of one or two newspapers and choose four different sports.
Read reports of games in each sport and copy out the words that belong to that sport alone.
Make a list of words for each sport.

22 Here is a description of an island. Read it and then draw a map of the island.

The island was almost circular in shape. In the west there was a deep bay. In the east the coast jutted out, and in the part that jutted out there was a hill. A stream ran from this hill to the bay in the west. In the south of the island a few houses clustered round a little church. In the north there was an old castle surrounded by tall trees. The only road on the island ran from the castle to the village. It crossed a bridge about half way along the stream.

Things

'Hullo,' said Roger. 'Somebody must be living here. Look at that.'

A thick cloud of yellow smoke had poured suddenly out from the top of a rusty iron pipe that stuck up through the deck close by the ancient windlass. Knee deep in the rank grass of the dyke, they stood and stared and sniffed the pungent smell. There could be no doubt about it. One end of the wreck was derelict, but the other end was still in use. That new tar in the bows, the new paint on the name, and now this smoke from the chimney, showed that, even if the *Speedy* would never sail again, even if it was only a matter of time before most of her would fall apart and disappear in the mud, someone still had a use for part of her. One end of her was wholly dead, but the other was very much alive. It was as if they had come across a skeleton and on looking at the skull had been greeted with a wink.

Arthur Ransome
Secret Water

The aeroplane dropped three bombs, or four bombs, or five bombs according to the day of the week. Their bursts of dense smoke sat on the sage-green plain compactly like cream puffs, writhing for minutes in the windless air before they slowly spread and faded. Though we knew there was no menace in it, yet we could not but catch our breath when the sharp-growing cry of falling bombs came through the loud engine overhead.

T E Lawrence
Seven Pillars of Wisdom

Questions to answer

'"Hullo," said Roger . . .'

1 Use a dictionary to write out the meaning of each of the following words:

windlass rank dyke pungent
derelict bows

2 What three things made the children think there was someone living in part of the boat?

3 Which part of the *Speedy* was derelict? Was it the bow, the port or left side, the stern, or the starboard or right side.
Give a reason for your answer.

4 Two of the senses are used in the description of the smoke coming from the rusty iron pipe. Which two senses are they?

5 How was the *Speedy* expected to meet her end?

6 What is the connection between the description of the *Speedy* and the last sentence?

'The aeroplane dropped . . .'

7 In your own words explain the pattern of bombing.

8 What do you learn about the attacker from the pattern of bombing?

9 '. . . bursts of dense smoke sat on the sage-green plain compactly like cream puffs.'
Read page 121 and then write a comment about this piece of imagery.

10 How does the writer describe the sound of falling bombs?

11 Is the description of the sound of falling bombs a good one? Compare it with the sound you have heard in war films on television.

12 The word *writhing* means 'to twist'. It is said that most words beginning with the letters WR deal with movement, e.g. *wrench* means 'to pull violently with a twisting movement'. Find FIVE other words that begin with WR and are about movement. Give a meaning for each one.

Writing

13 Write an account, as seen from the ground, of the dropping of supplies by parachute to soldiers, or to stranded animals or refugees.

14 Using the style of T E Lawrence, write a paragraph of about 70 words on:
(a) the detonation of an explosive charge
(b) a new car
(c) a mower cutting grass

15 'Great flames shot up like red and yellow spears against the black and starless sky.' Copy out this sentence and then continue for another 300 words with a description or a story.

16 Write a clear description of an orange in not more than 50 words.

17 Describe how you made something, either at home, or in the woodwork/metalwork/art/pottery/home economics rooms.

18 You have the opportunity to plan the layout of a spare room for your own use. Say what you would use the room for and describe how you would go about planning and equipping it.

Language—sentences

19 Some of the groups of words below are sentences and some are not. Write out those which are sentences.

Did you see the satellite last night
All the pupils in her class
He stopped
Ran out of the dark tunnel
The doctor promised to call once a week
Where to go or what to do
That clock is ten minutes fast
A walk through the park in the winter sunshine
During the last week of the summer holidays
Sandra did not know which bus to catch

Write out the groups of words you have left and for each group add enough (at the beginning, in the middle, or at the end) to turn it into a complete sentence.

20 Here are some sentences in which the capital letters and full stops have been missed out. Write the sentences as they should be.

suddenly the bow string twanged again the white stallion snorted and pawed the air in agony as the mortally stricken creature whirled about it brought the pony down geoffrey rolled clear of the flailing hooves but saw his sister fall from her mount and lie still

21 Rewrite the following nine sentences in their correct order to form a clear and sensible paragraph. There is no need to alter any words, only the order of the sentences.

The mustard is sown in the same way, three days later. For each, you need a small patch or box of fine soil. If you use a pair of scissors, you will avoid collecting earth with the mustard and cress. You can easily buy plain or curled cress seed and white mustard seed. Then sow a patch about one foot square with cress seed, sprinkling it fairly thickly on the surface, or covering it very lightly with more fine earth. It is a good idea to cover both seed-beds with brown paper for about four days, until the seed begins to grow. If necessary sift the soil through a garden sieve, discarding stones and lumps. Mustard and cress is a popular salad crop that is easy to grow. When the crops are about three or four inches high, you can begin cutting them for salads.

22 Make the sentences in each of the following groups into ONE complete sentence *in the best and most sensible way you can*. Write ONE complete sentence for each group.

(a) Father and I went to the circus
We saw many animals
They were clever animals

(b) The camper built a fire
He mixed some dough
He made bread-rolls for his supper

(c) Bees visit flowers
They go in search of nectar
The bees get nectar with their long, sucking tongues

(d) The bank cashier counted the notes on to her desk
She snapped a rubber band around them
She pushed them across to the customer

Learning at home

23 Imagine you watched a film on television whilst you were alone in the house. Someone comes in and the following conversation takes place.

'How was the film?'
'Very good.'
'What was it about, then?'

Finish this conversation by telling in not more than 200 words the story of any film you have seen on television.

24 Tell, in not more than 150 words, the story of the last book you read at home.

25 In life you come across some things you like and others you dislike. Write about ONE of the following topics and say in detail what you like and dislike.
(a) food (b) sounds (c) games
(d) music (e) colours

Nature

There was a little sunshine now, not much warmth in it, but it made things look brighter, especially the small pools of ice in the gutters . . . Itchy Park was an old graveyard . . . At Itchy Park the sun made the white stone pillars and whitened headstones shine like alabaster . . . Some of the crocuses were shooting and striped dark green leaves showed through the grass which was winter thin and short. One of the crocuses was quite large but it looked as if it would never flower and felt stone cold. In spite of the sun, blasts of wind cut through the graveyard like wet stone knives. It was no wonder if the flowers were frozen stiff, and the glass thin, and the angels splitting.

Wolf Mankowitz
A Kid for Two Farthings

I saw a small black snake, about eighteen inches long, slowly swallowing a lizard.—The head and shoulders of the lizard had already disappeared and we could just see the tips of its front toes, pressed back against its body, projecting out of the corners of the snake's mouth. In girth, the snake was about a third of the size of the lizard, and to accommodate its enormous meal, the snake had unhinged its lower jaw. Even so, it had to open its mouth so wide that its little black eyes almost popped out of its head . . .

David Attenborough
The Snake

In certain low, bare, grey, wrinkled volcanic hills huge vultures make a home, spying from afar the tired camel which will inevitably drop out of the caravan line and sink by the track not to rise again, or the overladen mule or donkey which is losing strength in the howling blizzard and will soon be frozen to death.

Far overhead Golden Eagles and buzzards outline wide curves in the clear sky, and below them the sparrow-hawk hovers, ready to swoop on any small rodent which has ventured into the open. Among the salt marshes grey herons feed on lizards, and sometimes, where a quiet oasis has a few trees, the branches will be covered with the angular forms of these birds. . . .

Mildred Cable and Francesca French
Gobi Desert

Grass snake eating frog

Questions to answer

Find answers to the following questions in the three passages on page 34.

Write your answers in complete sentences.

1 What effect did the sun have on the pillars and headstones at Itchy Park?
2 How did the small snake manage to get the large meal into its mouth?
3 Where did the huge vultures make their home?
4 How much larger was the lizard than the snake?
5 What made the grass in Itchy Park thin and short?
6 Name three animals on which the huge vultures fed.
7 What made the angels in the churchyard split?
8 Name four birds, other than the huge vultures, that were also hunting for food in the Gobi Desert.
9 Had you been watching the snake eat the lizard would you have seen the tail hanging from the snake's mouth at this stage?
10 The sun was shining in Itchy Park but there had been a frost. How do we know this?
11 What tells us there was a trade route running through this part of the Gobi Desert?
12 Observation and description play a part in all these passages. Which one do you think is the best? Give your reasons.

Wings spread and dropped slightly.

Primaries
Dark sooty brown.

Creamy white base of primaries and all coverts *

All streaks and spots - dark sooty brown

Legs and toes pale chrome yellow. Claws black

KESTREL (Female)

Beginning descent from hover. At last moment claws will open to grasp prey.

* covert — a feather covering the quill-bases of wings and tail.

Writing

13 Study the picture and information on the opposite page.
Write down as much as you can about the appearance and behaviour of a kestrel.

14 Write a story called 'The Snake'.

15 It is very late and the night is dark.
From the bottom of your garden comes a scuffling sound.
You are brave enough to go out to see what is going on.
Describe what you find.

16 Write a letter answering the following advertisement:

Breed butterflies at home! Many species and simple equipment shown in our catalogue. Write for our latest to Worldwide Butterflies Ltd, Nether Compton, Shorburn, Dorset.

17 Describe a time when you were impressed or frightened by the *power* of nature.
You might, for example, tell of being caught in a violent thunderstorm.

18 Write a short description of a cat stalking a bird.

Talking

19 Be ready, when asked, to bring to school some part of nature.
You will be asked to describe it, to explain what it is and why you chose to bring it, and then to answer questions about it.

Exotic pets – a slippery African house snake

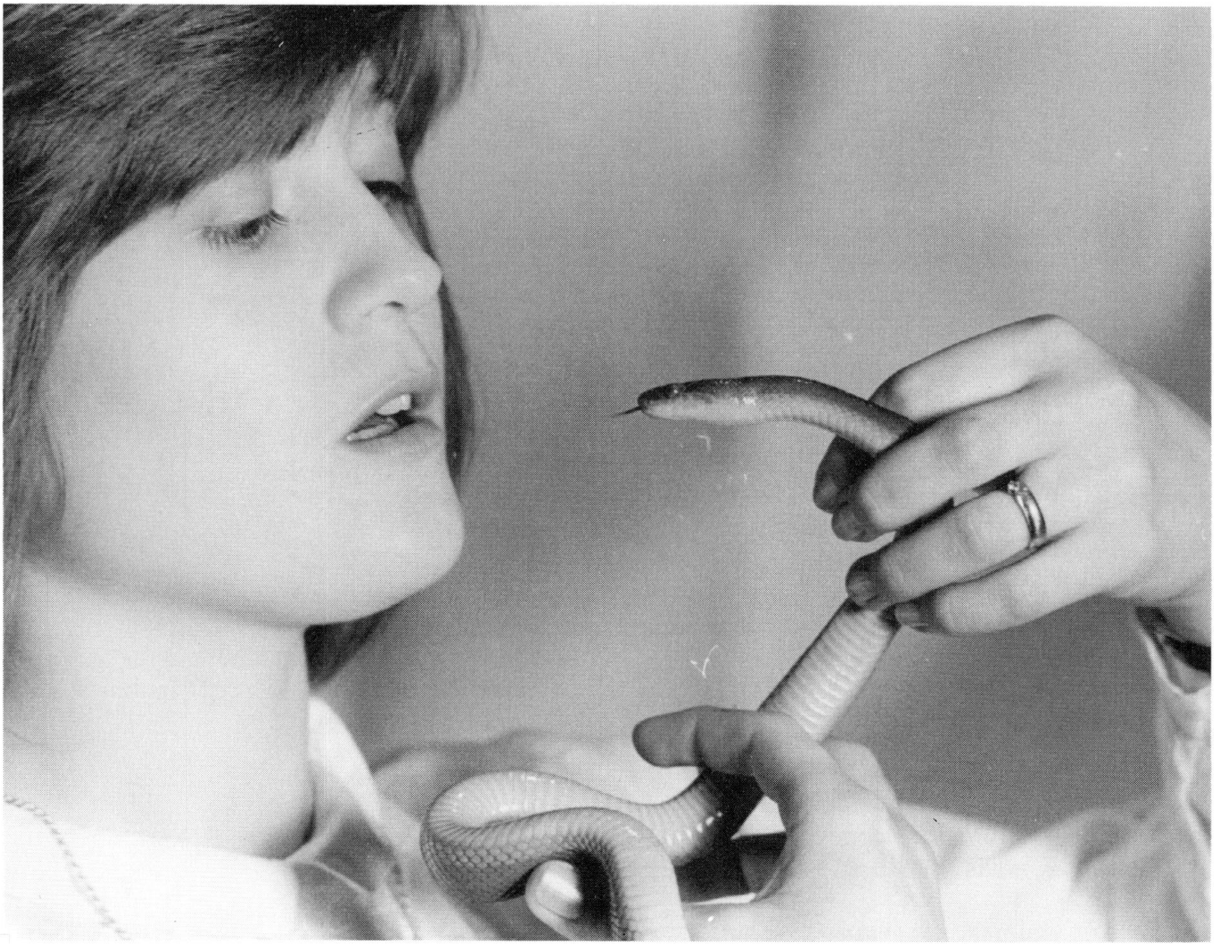

An inquisitive leopard gecko

A mysterious millipede

A tricky red-kneed tarantula

20 Organise a class discussion about threats to wildlife. The following may give you some ideas:

We often behave as if animals and plants have no right to exist on earth.
We destroy their homes by cutting down woods and forests.
We poison animals with pesticides.
We kill animals for food such as turtle soup.
We kill animals for expensive products like tiger-skin coats and crocodile-skin shoes and handbags.
Do we really need all these things?
Who needs a tiger-skin coat more—a rich woman or a tiger?

Language—the colon

The punctuation mark (:) is called a colon. It is used to:

introduce lists of items

e.g. Alan was first-class at five games: cricket, tennis, football, badminton and golf.
Louise sent party invitations to the following friends: John, Cheryl, Brendan, Denise, Leslie and Melanie.

introduce a quotation or extract
e.g. As Mark Twain wrote in *Pudd'nhead Wilson's Calendar*: 'When angry, count four; when very angry, swear.'
He suddenly shouted: 'Get out of here! Get out, I tell you!'

introduce a conclusion to a sentence
e.g. We weighed up the situation, thought for a while, and then did the only thing we could: ran as fast as possible from the danger.

add further information
e.g. He was not feeling well: severe pain was creeping up both legs.

Use the information given above to help you write out and punctuate the following.

There is a colon to be placed in each sentence.

21 (a) he ended with the words i have nothing further to say gentlemen
(b) there is a proverb too many cooks spoil the broth
(c) a soldier needs many qualities courage strength skill and intelligence
(d) george grossmith wrote in his the diary of a nobody whats the use of a home if you are never in it
(e) the chief exports of spain are fruit foodstuffs wine minerals and textiles
(f) the following was found in the dead mans pockets a wallet containing five ten pound notes seventy five pence in small change an empty cigarette packet and a return coach ticket to canterbury
(g) the motto of 18 squadron in the royal air force was with courage and faith
(h) be sure when you are packing for camp you have everything you need tent stove sleeping bag cooler and fishing rod
(i) she reminded him of the words of alexander pope a little learning is a dangerous thing

Learning at home

22 Find a wildlife picture that appeals to you. Paste on paper and write about whatever it suggests to you.

23 Imagine you have been asked to write an article about ONE of the following for a magazine called *Wildlife*.

badgers tawny owls ants
harvest mice

Find out as much as you can about your choice from books in the school and public libraries. Make notes and work out the best way to present your writing.
Write the article in YOUR OWN WORDS.

24 Spend some time watching a pet or any animal you know. Describe as well as you can its appearance and its behaviour.

Half-Past Morning on an Autumn Day

I was walking by the Thames. Half-past morning on an autumn day. Sun in a mist. Like an orange in a fried fish shop. All bright below. Low tide, dusty water and a crooked bar of straw, chicken boxes, dirt and oil from mud to mud. Like a viper swimming in skim milk. The old serpent, symbol of nature and love . . .

The sun had crackled into flames at the top; the mist was getting thin in places, you could see crooked lines of grey, like old cracks under spring ice. Tide on the turn. Snake broken up. Emeralds and sapphires. Water like varnish with bits of gold leaf floating thick and heavy. Gold is the metal of intellect. And all at once the sun burned through in a new place, at the side, and shot out a ray that hit the Eagle and Child, next the motor boat factory, right on the new signboard.

Joyce Cary
The Horse's Mouth

Questions to answer

1 Explain 'Half-past morning' in your own words.
2 The writer says that the sun in mist on an autumn morning looks 'Like an orange in a fried fish shop.'
Say why you do or do not think this a good simile (see page 119).
3 What was it that (a) looked like a viper, and (b) looked like skim milk?
4 How do we know the mist was thinning in places?
5 'Snake broken up.'
What was happening to the river and its bar of straw, chicken boxes, dirt and oil?
6 What made the water look like 'Emeralds and sapphires'?
7 How do we know the sun was shining before it 'burned through in a new place'?
8 What was the 'Eagle and Child'?

Language—similes

Like an orange in a fried fish shop
Like a viper swimming in skim milk

These are similes.

Writers use them to place very clear pictures in the minds of their readers.

9 Make a list of all similes in the passage. For each one say what is being compared.

For example, the sun in a mist is compared with an orange in a fried fish shop.

10 Make a list of the sights, sounds and smells of a river. Arrange your words under the three headings.

11 Write some similes of your own to help others see each of the following quite clearly:
(a) the blue, bitter smoke of wood
(b) the red, setting sun on a summer's evening
(c) the lights of a fairground
(d) the darkness on a pitch-black night
(e) moonlight on a bottle in a ditch

12 Use each of the following words in a simile.

cream fruit temple avalanche
harvest hurricane

Writing

13 Write a passage similar to the one by Joyce Cary about the following.
(a) a churchyard at dawn
(b) wet roofs and pavements beneath the lamplight
(c) the sea at high tide

14 Describe the scene on page 40 in not more than 300 words.
Try to make the reader feel he/she is there by adding the sounds, smells and sensations which are not in the picture.

15 Write a descriptive essay about a walk in the rain.

16 Study very carefully the picture below.
Your task is to describe it as *completely* as you can in just three sentences.
Make notes of all the information you need before you start to write the sentences.

Learning at home

17 Find a small area (about one square metre) of your garden or local playing field or park.
It could be part of a fence, a brick wall, a tree trunk, a flower bed or a path.
Study it carefully for some time.
Make a note of *everything* you see—colours, shapes, living things, texture, etc.
Try to describe what you see as precisely as possible.
Write an accurate description of the area.

3 Narration

Language for narration is about action. It lets the reader know what is happening by telling a story. If language for description is like a photograph, then language for narration is like a moving photograph or film.

The point of view from which a story is told is important. The two main points of view are the first and the third person. In the first person, an 'I' tells of an event in which *he* or *she* is taking part. In the third person an author writes of an event about another person.

Contents

GOPAL AND THE HILSA-FISH
IT WAS THE SEASON FOR HILSA-FISH. FISHERMEN COULD THINK OF NOTHING BUT HILSA-FISH.
FISHMONGERS SOLD NOTHING BUT HILSA-FISH.
COME, BUY. THE PRICE OF HILSA IS DOWN TODAY.
HOUSEHOLDERS COULD TALK OF NOTHING BUT HILSA-FISH.
HOW MUCH DID YOU PAY FOR THAT HILSA ?
YOU WOULDN'T BELIEVE IT IF I TOLD YOU.
AND IN THE PALACE TOO THE COURTIERS COULD DISCUSS NOTHING BUT HILSA-FISH.
YOUR MAJESTY, YOU SHOULD HAVE SEEN THE HUGE HILSA I CAUGHT. IT WAS...

STOP IT!
ARE YOU A COURTIER OR A FISHERMAN?
THE COURTIER FELL SILENT WITH DOWNCAST EYES. THE KING FELT GUILTY.
I'M SORRY I LOST MY TEMPER. IT IS THE SEASON FOR HILSA-FISH AND NO ONE...
...NOT EVEN GOPAL CAN STOP ANYONE FROM TALKING ABOUT HILSA-FISH. NOT EVEN FOR FIVE MINUTES!
OH, I THINK I COULD, YOUR MAJESTY.
THEN LET ME SEE YOU BUY A HUGE HILSA AND BRING IT TO THE PALACE WITHOUT ANYONE ASKING YOU A WORD ABOUT IT!
I ACCEPT THE CHALLENGE, YOUR MAJESTY.

A FEW DAYS LATER—
WHY IS YOUR FACE HALF-SHAVEN?
I'M DRESSING UP TO BUY A FISH.
WHAT'S THE MATTER WITH YOU? WHY ARE YOU SMEARING YOURSELF WITH ASH?
I TOLD YOU— I'M DRESSING UP TO BUY A HILSA-FISH.
LISTEN TO ME! PLEASE. YOU CAN'T POSSIBLY GO OUT IN THOSE DISGRACEFUL RAGS! WHAT ARE YOU UP TO?
HOW MANY TIMES MUST I TELL YOU, WOMAN? I AM OUT TO BUY A HUGE HILSA-FISH.
IT'S HAPPENED TO HIM! HE'S GONE MAD!

GOPAL BOUGHT THE HILSA-FISH AND STARTED WALKING TOWARDS THE PALACE.
MOTHER, LOOK AT THAT MAN! ISN'T HE COMICAL?
HE MUST BE A MADMAN.
HUSH! I THINK HE'S A MYSTIC.
WHEN GOPAL REACHED THE COURT—
WHAT DO YOU WANT?
I WANT TO SEE THE KING!
YOU CAN'T SEE THE KING! GET AWAY WITH YOU!
GOPAL BEGAN TO DANCE AND SING LOUDLY.

INSIDE THE PALACE—
THE MAN IS CRAZY !
THROW HIM OUT AT ONCE !
I WANT TO SEE THE KING. LET ME IN!
BRING THAT MAN TO ME AT ONCE !
YES, YOUR MAJESTY.
GOPAL WAS BROUGHT BEFORE THE KING.
IT'S GOPAL !
THE MAN HAS LOST HIS MIND !
I THINK IT'S ONE OF HIS CRAZY JOKES.

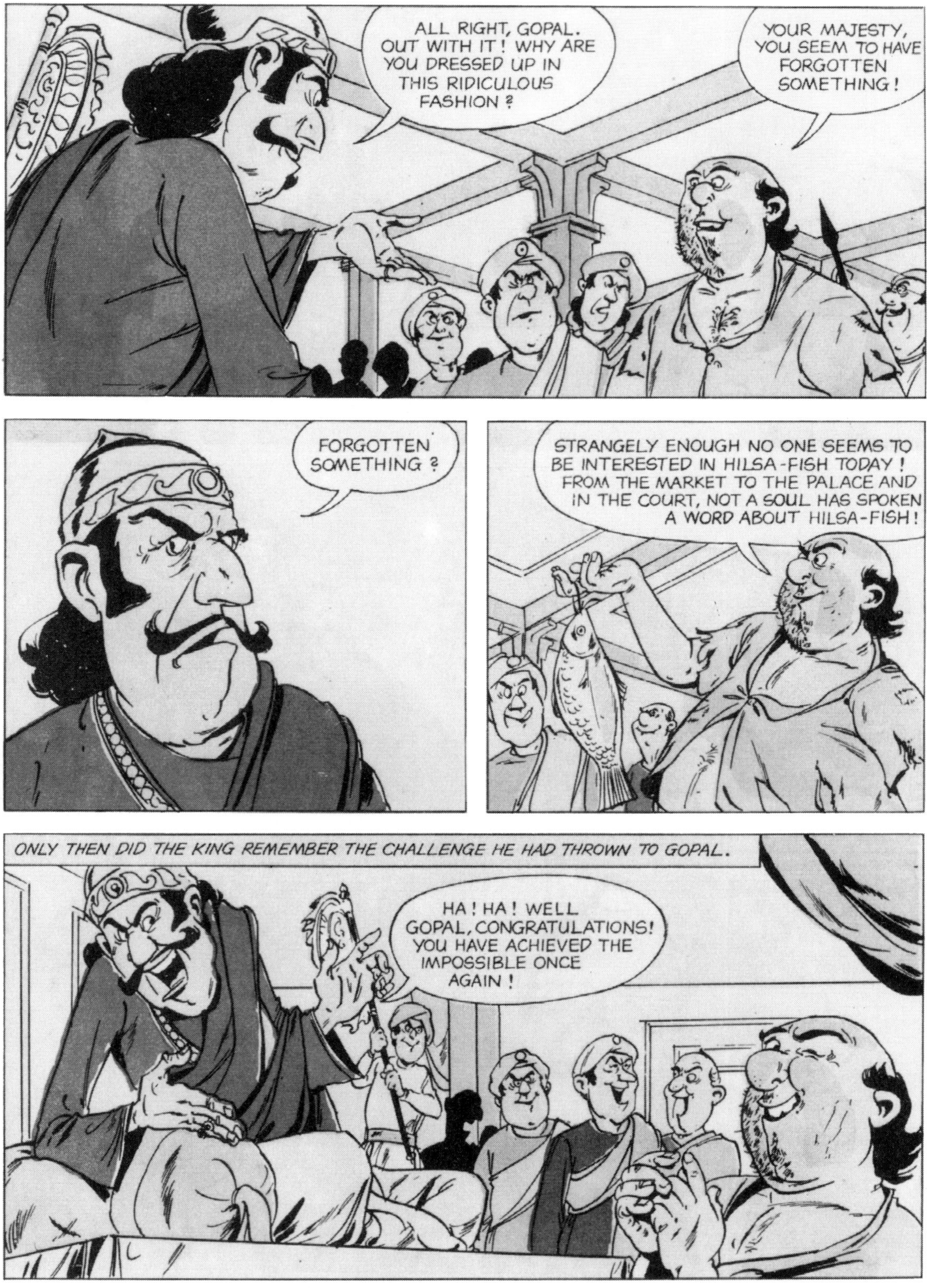
ALL RIGHT, GOPAL. OUT WITH IT! WHY ARE YOU DRESSED UP IN THIS RIDICULOUS FASHION ?
YOUR MAJESTY, YOU SEEM TO HAVE FORGOTTEN SOMETHING!
FORGOTTEN SOMETHING ?
STRANGELY ENOUGH NO ONE SEEMS TO BE INTERESTED IN HILSA-FISH TODAY! FROM THE MARKET TO THE PALACE AND IN THE COURT, NOT A SOUL HAS SPOKEN A WORD ABOUT HILSA-FISH!
ONLY THEN DID THE KING REMEMBER THE CHALLENGE HE HAD THROWN TO GOPAL.
HA! HA! WELL GOPAL, CONGRATULATIONS! YOU HAVE ACHIEVED THE IMPOSSIBLE ONCE AGAIN!

Questions to answer

1 Who are the *important* people in this story?
2 Where does the story take place?
3 At which time of the year does the story happen?
4 When does the action of the story take place? Is it in the past or in the present or in the future?
5 What *kind* of story is this? Is it an adventure story, a love story, a school story, a comic story or what?
6 How does the story end?

Language—narration

Narrate: to describe events in order,
to give an account of something,
to tell a story

Narrative: telling a story or having the form of a story,
a narrative essay or a narrative poem (see page 130)

So, a narrative essay is one that tells a story.

It describes events in order.

To place events in order a plan is needed.

The plot (the outline of what happens in a story) can then be thought out properly.

The story may be about anything, but it must be interesting. Get the reader interested from the start and keep that interest going until the end.

Think of the plot as a length of thread that may twist and turn but the spell for the reader must not be broken.

7 Telling the story of your life at school is a good way to practise placing events in their correct order.
Start with the date and place of your birth and go on to tell of your earliest memories.
Follow this with experiences at playgroup, nursery and first school. How did you manage being away from mother? Did you run away from school?
Who were the people you met and what were they like? Was there a Wendy House or sand or water or toys to play with?
Next come the years at middle school. What do you remember best about these? What were the highlights? Lessons? Visits? Things you took part in? Who are the people you remember from that time?
Lastly, your move to secondary school. How did you feel on that first day? What has happened since that stays in your memory?
Write your story and call it 'My life at school'.

8 Choose THREE of the following titles and think how you can build each one into a story.
Make a brief plan for each title by asking the six questions under 'Questions to answer' on page 49.

Lost on the hills
Race against time
Fire in the night
The accident
The Viking ship
Waiting at the bus stop

9 Work out the outline of a story about either (a) a girl with very long hair that caused her trouble, or (b) the face at the window.

10 The shortest person in the world was a Dutch girl called Pauline Musters. When she died she was just 58 cm (23 inches) high. Imagine you knew Pauline. Complete these sentences about her.
(a) I would (or would not) like Pauline living with me because . . .
(b) I would (or would not) take Pauline to school with me because . . .
(c) I would (or would not) like to be Pauline's size because . . .

11 Imagine you were Pauline (see question 10). Write the story of your life and adventures.

Writing

12 Imagine you bought several giant balloons filled with gas. As you carried them home

they began to lift you into the air and carry you away. Tell the story of what happened.

13 Write an interesting story about a woman who was found throwing £20 notes from a bridge into a river.

14 Imagine you were sleeping in a room when you were visited by a ghost in the early hours of the morning. The ghost told you the story of why it haunted the house. Write that story for others to read.

Learning at home

15 Give TWO possible meanings for EACH of the following sentences.
   (a) The headmaster will expel all pupils he thinks fit.
   (b) A queue of single people stood outside the cinema.
   (c) She buys Chelson's cheese because she knows no better.
   (d) Whilst reading your letter I was completely lost.
   (e) Trespassers leaving the gates open will force the farmer to bar them.

16 Add either IN, UN or DIS to the root word so that it has the opposite meaning. The first is done for you.

Root words	*Opposite*
visible	invisible
dress	
fit	
fortunate	
occupied	
comfortable	
obey	
able	
direct	
interested	
honest	
armed	
significant	
edible	

Call Me Silky

Silky was a young man of seventy when I first met him, and the time when he would be reduced to vaulting a five-bar gate instead of jumping it clean was ten years' distant. He walked slowly round me as I stood outside the back door of his farm where we were evacuated, and shook his white head appreciatively. I held a shotgun in one hand and a crook in the other and tried to look useful. I thought I was being very successful.

'How old are you, boy?' he asked suddenly.

'Nine,' I said proudly, knowing I was big for my age.

'Nine,' he said wonderingly. 'Nine.' I had a feeling that he wasn't too satisfied with me. 'D'you know, boy, there's something wrong with you and I can't figure what.' He went on circling me, muttering to himself.

Then he straightened up and slapped his thigh. 'I've got it!' he said. 'I've got it!'

I looked at him.

'No whiskers, of course.' He stood stroking his glossy white moustache. 'No whiskers, that'd be it.'

He shot a piercing glance. 'Now listen, boy; it's a very peculiar thing for a nine-year-old man not to have whiskers, and I don't want you discussing this with the women. Got that?'

'Y-yes,' I said.

'Not with your Mum, not my wife your Aunt Mary. 'Cos I'll tell you for why. This is a man's job, and women are always interfering with man's jobs, my boy.' And he snarled at the kitchen where the two women could be fancied to be.

'Yes, Mr Harris,' I said.

'Don't call me Mr Harris. Call me Silky. Everyone does.'

'Yes, Silky.'

'"Silky, sir" to a man of nine!'

'Yes, Silky, sir.'

'Well now, boy, there's only one cure for your predicament, and luckily for you I know what it is. I suffered from the same complaint myself. I was gone ten when I managed to grow these.' And he stroked his whiskers again.

'What have I got to do, Silky?'

'Sir!'

'Sir.'

'You'll have to get up real early, boy, farmer's early, and fill up your shoes with sheep's dung.'

I gasped.

'And mind you, I say early because it's got to be dung with the dew on it. Sheep's dung, see! That's how they grow all that wool.'

I nodded, breathless.

'And that's not all. It's mucky stuff, as you probably know. So don't wear any socks. A woman won't wash socks even if a man's whiskers are at stake. And you'll need a silver spoon.'

'A silver spoon, Silky?'

'A silver spoon, sir.'

'Sir.'

'Yes, a silver spoon to load the dung into your boots.'

'Where will I get a silver spoon.'

'You'll get one off your Aunt Mary!' He snarled once more at the kitchen. 'And don't come crying to me for help if they catch you. I've got my whiskers.'

After a while I returned with the spoon.

'Hide it, boy. Guard it with your life. Now listen. Creep out at six tomorrow morning into that near meadow and select your dung carefully. A fresh pile will be jet black. Got that?'

I nodded.

'Then fill your boots alternately—one spoonful in one and one in the other. Make sure you lace them up good and tight. You'll have your whiskers in no time at all. When you've grown 'em you can come rabbit shooting. Till then you're too conspicuous to the rabbits.'

'Is that why you're so good, Silky?'

'That's right, boy.' His son and two grandsons shot clay pigeons for England. He picked up his gun and walked out of the farmyard.

[*The boy carries out Silky's instructions but there are still no whiskers at the end of the day.*]

The evening meal was a happier one for everyone except me. My mother stopped sniffing, and my aunt no longer looked furtive. Silky said he was going shooting in the morning, so we'd have a game dinner. I knew he wouldn't take me without my whiskers.

I didn't exactly cry. When the meal was over I went up to Silky as he oiled his gun.

'You're a queer case,' he said.

I nodded sadly.

'Sheep's dung?'

'Yes.'

'Fresh?'

'Yes. I saw the sheep . . .'

'That's enough of that, boy. There are women in the house. Dew on it?'

'Yes.'

'Both sides?'

'I-I think so, Silky.'

'Sir!'

'Sir.'

'I've never heard the like. They did the same thing for a bald baby down the road and it worked a treat. How old are you?'

'Nine.'

'Older than the baby. Come over here to the light, boy. Come over here to the light.' He was looking unhappy, too. 'It's the shooting tomorrow, d'you see?'

'I know, Silky.'

'I won't ask you to say "sir". I can see you're very upset. Open your mouth.'

I opened my mouth and his white whiskered face came down to mine as he looked inside with first one eye and then the other. 'Well I'll be darned,' he said suddenly, slapping his knee. 'Well I'll be darned. I've heard of it, but I've never seen it. Queerest case I've come across.'

I looked at him agog.

'One thing's sure. You can get ready to come shooting tomorrow. That's certain enough. Poor little beggar.' And he went back to oiling his gun.

'B-but what's up, Silky?'

'Nothing's up, boy. That's the point. You've got your whiskers there right enough. Very likely had 'em from birth, if you belong to a hairy family. The thing is, boy, you've been gnawing them off inside, and they've never had a chance. Remarkable teeth you've got. It's a clear case of ingrowing whiskers.'

'But, Silky . . .'

'Don't you say a word more, boy—especially to the women. They'd be jealous. Ingrowing whiskers—that's it.'

Michael Baldwin
Grandad with Snails

Questions to answer

1 *Where* does this story take place?
2 *When* does the story take place?
3 How old would Silky be before he was 'reduced to vaulting a five-bar gate'?
4 Why was Silky not satisfied after he had inspected the boy?
5 Why was the boy ordered not to discuss his problem with the women in the house?
6 Explain the difference between getting up early and getting up 'farmer's early'.
7 Why was sheep's dung good for growing whiskers?
8 How would the boy know that the sheep's dung was fresh?
9 The boy was told to get up early and find sheep's dung with dew on it. What other instructions were given by Silky to the boy?
10 What did you find out about (a) Silky, and (b) the boy, in the first 20 lines?
11 Why were whiskers needed when rabbit shooting?
12 What did Silky finally decide was wrong with the boy?
13 Give reasons why you think Silky was playing a game with the boy.
14 What does Baldwin say in the first sentence to surprise you?
15 What sort of story do you think this is?
16 How would you expect this story to continue?

Language—narration: how to begin

Silky was a young man of seventy when I first met him . . .
We do not expect men of seventy to be called young nor to be able to jump over a five-bar gate.

This sentence is used to interest the reader and make him want to find out more about that athletic senior citizen.

A few lines later we learn where the story is set and when it takes place. We are also interested in a plot that is beginning to unfold.

All this needs to be given at the start of any story. The rules are:

(a) interest the reader with the opening sentences, and
(b) introduce as quickly as you can, the characters, the place, the time and the situation.

17 Here are the opening sentences for three stories.
(a) My name is Sharon Derby and I'm thirteen. It doesn't show because I look like an underdone angel.
(b) Mum had sent me out to get an extra pail of air. I'd just about filled it when I saw the thing.
(c) Mum and Dad were fighting again, not really angry with each other, but arguing very loud. They had been at it, off and on, for weeks.

All three have interesting openings that introduce a character or characters.
Write out three other opening sentences that bring in, as quickly as possible, a place for the story, a time for the story and the situation.

Writing

18 Imagine you are going to write a story about the area in which you live.
Write an opening paragraph that describes the area and hints at what the story is about. Do not make it a long paragraph.
19 Write an exciting introduction for two of the following stories:

The last man
Underwater adventure
Cattle stampede
The quarrel

20 Write two opening sentences for a story of your own choosing. Make the sentences interesting but at the same time introduce one or more characters.
21 Write a short story that uses the picture on page 55.
22 Write about a time when you had your leg pulled or someone made a fool of you. How did it feel?
23 Imagine you are a grandparent. Write a letter of advice to your grandchild.

Talking and listening

24 *Class discussion*: People of different ages will always quarrel.

25 Form groups of four.
Spend some time working out the following situation.
Two members of the group are suspects accused of a murder and the other two are detectives. The suspects are given a few minutes to set up a joint alibi to cover the two hours during which the murder was committed.
The detectives set out to break the alibi by questioning the suspects one at a time and then together.

Learning at home

26 Talk to a grandparent, or someone of Silky's age, about their schooldays.
Make a note of what is said or tape record the talk. Be sure to ask if the tape recorder may be used.
Write an account of how education has changed since that person was at school.

27 What do we call people who live in the following districts, places or countries?

e.g. Sweden—Swedish

Spain	Wales
Norway	Peru
Switzerland	Crete
Belgium	Scotland
Cuba	Manchester
Cyprus	Devon
Finland	Lancashire
Iceland	Hawaii
Portugal	Brittany

28 The following words have at least two different meanings. For each word write two sentences that show those meanings.

e.g. *instant*
(a) My mother doesn't like instant coffee.
(b) People had gathered within an instant of the accident happening.

sound	flag	sentence	service
hamper	season	tender	scale
mould	steep		

No Other Trace Has Been Discovered

Then she heard a curious noice. It was quite soft at first. It sounded like someone or something panting very quickly. She turned. There was nothing. The sound seemed to be following her, getting steadily louder.

It was soon joined by another sound: the pad, pad, pad of feet, like the paws of an animal. It appeared to be at the side of the road, moving at a constant speed. Very frightened by this time, she turned and saw a dark shape by the hedge. All was silent except for the panting and the incessant pad, pad, pad. She began to cry a little. Wasn't there a phone box about? But there was no phone; not even a house in sight.

She stopped. The panting stopped. The padding ceased. Absolute silence again. Then, as the moon came out from behind the clouds, she saw the black shape clearly. There it stood, a dog, a huge dog, black as the night that surrounded it. Only two things shone out in the darkness—its eyes that glowed like fire, and the white of its teeth bared in a snarl.

Mary Danby (ed.)
11th Armada Ghost Book

There was a death in the paddock. For nine days the police had followed a man's footsteps. Once and again the footmarks would turn back upon themselves. Now they would lead round and round a tree. Now they would shoot off at right angles. At long intervals the searchers had found towards evening clear signs that his feet had begun to drag. They could see clearly the long scrape of the toe before each heel-mark. They quickened pace, following the tracks with all the skill that was in them. Presently they came to his hat. There the dark closed in upon them. It was too black to follow, and they had to camp.

That night down came the rain. By the morning every trace of the tracks had been sponged away as from a slate. All day they searched —both the trooper and the black tracker—but they found nothing. Months later, a boundary rider came upon his coat. There were letters in it from some man in Scotland; from that day to this no other trace of him has been discovered.

C E W Bean
On the Wool Track

Questions to answer

Find answers to the following questions in the two passages above.
Write your answers in complete sentences.

1 What two noises did the girl hear behind her?
2 Why was the girl frightened at this time?
3 The man the police were tracking was tired and dragging his feet. How did the police know this?
4 Why did the police quicken their pace?
5 What made the girl cry a little?
6 What did the police find that showed they

were on the right track?

7 Why did the police decide to camp when they were getting near?

8 How were the man's tracks wiped out?

9 Who searched for the man once his tracks had been wiped out?

10 Why is the word 'pad' used so often in the first passage?

11 What evidence is there that the event in the second passage took place in Australia?

12 Was the dog who followed the girl an ordinary or a supernatural one? Give reasons for your answer.

13 Which three items belonging to the man were recovered?

14 Supply titles for both passages.

Writing

15 Write a beginning and an ending for the passage about the girl.

16 Write a story about the man in the paddock, who he was, where he came from and what happened to him.

17 Build a story around the picture below.

18 Look into one of the windows opposite. What story do you see? Tell it.

Language

19 Here is the writer James Joyce having fun with words. Try to puzzle out what is happening.

Rats! bullowed the Mookse most telesphorously, the concionator, and the sissymusses and the zozzymusses in their robenhauses quailed to hear his tardeynoise at all for you cannot wake a silken nouse out of a hoarseoar. Blast yourself and your anathomy infairioriboos! No, hang you for an animal rurale! I am superbly in my supremest poncif! Abase you, baldyqueens! Gather behind me, satraps! Rots!

Write a similar piece in which someone or something is talking angrily to a group.

20 Twelve words have been taken out of this passage and the gaps numbered.
Write down the numbers 1–12 and then read the passage.

He had not been long in this (1) . . . when he was strangely disturbed. The (2) . . . in that upper storey of the house was only broken by the (3) . . . of the flames and the hissing of a wet (4) . . . in the hearth; but presently, to Dick's strained (5) . . ., there came the sound of someone (6) . . . with extreme caution; and soon after the door (7) . . ., and a little pale-faced dwarf pushed first his (8) . . . and then his crooked body into the (9) . . .. His mouth was open as (10) . . . to hear the better; and his (11) . . ., which were very bright, (12) . . . restlessly and swiftly to and fro.

Choose from this list the correct word to write beside each of the numbers you have written down.

(1) basket bath position
(2) wind silence noise
(3) smoking tramp crackling
(4) cricket sweep log
(5) hearing ankle appetite
(6) snoring walking stamping
(7) latched closed open
(8) dog body head
(9) window chimney chamber
(10) though never although
(11) toes eyes teeth
(12) rest accelerated flitted

21 In the following passage put full stops, commas and capitals where you think they are needed.

christopher strode across the field he had no idea what he was going to find behind the hedge but he was determined not to turn back as he approached his heart was pounding and his knees felt weak suddenly a dog a strange one sprang out and challenged him the boy pushed it aside with his stick climbed the fence and jumped down the other side stood the stranger in his hand the stolen gun

22 Here are four prefixes with their meanings.
Write down three words which start with each.

bi (two) equi (equal)
dis (apart) mis (wrong)

Put six of your words into sentences.

23 A *homonym* is a word having the same sound, and sometimes spelling, as another but with a different meaning.

e.g. *dear* and *deer*

Here are some words that are alike in sound but different in spelling and meaning.
Explain how the words in each pair differ in meaning.

bail bale
beer bier
boar bore
braid brayed
bare bear
bell belle
brae bray
brake break
beach beech
bold bowled
bread bred

Learning at home

24 Write a letter to a friend in hospital telling about any book you have read.

25 Find out what you can about one of the following and make notes for a short talk on the subject to the remainder of the class.

How to attract butterflies to your garden
The natterjack toad
Brent Geese
Stinkhorns
Autumn ladies' tresses

I Have to Ask You to Come with Me

They arrested us after breakfast. We took a little walk through the village then went down to the quay to get our bags. A soldier was standing guard over the boat.

'Is this your boat?'

'Yes.'

'Where do you come from?'

'Up the lake.'

'Then I have to ask you to come with me.'

'How about the bags?'

'You can carry the bags.'

I carried the bags and Catherine walked beside me and the soldier walked along behind us to the old custom-house. In the custom-house a lieutenant, very thin and military, questioned us.

'What nationality are you?'

'American and British.'

'Let me see your passports.'

I gave him mine and Catherine got hers out of her handbag.

He examined them for a long time.

'Why do you enter Switzerland this way in a boat?'

'I am a sportsman,' I said. 'Rowing is my great sport. I always row when I get a chance.'

'Why do you come here?'

'For the winter sport. We are tourists and we want to do the winter sport.'

'This is no place for winter sport.'

'We know it. We want to go where they have the winter sport.'

'What have you been doing in Italy?'

'I have been studying architecture. My cousin has been studying art.'

'Why do you leave there?'

'We want to do the winter sport. With the war going on you cannot study architecture.'

'You will please stay where you are,' the lieutenant said. He went back into the building with our passports.

'You're splendid, darling,' Catherine said. 'Keep on the same track. You want to do the winter sport.'

'Do you know anything about art?'

'Rubens,' said Catherine.

'Large and fat,' I said.

'Titian,' Catherine said.

'Titian-haired,' I said. 'How about Mantegna?'

'Don't ask hard ones,' Catherine said. 'I know him though—very bitter.'

'Very bitter,' I said. 'Lots of nail holes.'

'You see I'll make you a fine wife,' Catherine said. ' I'll be able to talk art with your customers.'

'Here he comes,' I said. The thin lieutenant came down the length of the custom-house, holding our passports.

'I will have to send you into Locarno,' he said. 'You can get a carriage and a soldier will go in with you.'

'All right,' I said. 'What about the boat?'

'The boat is confiscated.'

Ernest Hemingway
A Farewell to Arms

Questions to answer

1 Who had to carry the bags?
2 What rank was the officer who questioned the couple?
3 The two entered Switzerland by boat. What reason was given for so doing?
4 What explanation was given for coming to Switzerland?
5 Which country had the couple left?
6 Why was the man not able to study architecture?
7 Why was Catherine asked questions about art?
8 What kind of people were painted by Rubens?
9 Which four words lead us to think that Mantegna painted scenes of the crucifixion of Christ?
10 How do we know that the couple are not cousins?
11 Tell in your own words how the officer treated the two.
12 Here are meanings for three words in the passage. Which are the three words?
    (a) an official document of identification. (line 16)
    (b) a building in which business connected with taxes on imported goods is done. (line 48)
    (c) something belonging to another person is taken either with legal authority or as a punishment. (line 52)
13 Tell in your own words what this passage is about.

Language—dialogue

'Is this your boat?'
'Yes.'
'Where do you come from?'
'Up the lake.'
'Then I have to ask you to come with me.'

Conversation in print or writing is called *dialogue*.

The writing of dialogue looks very easy but there are one or two rules to follow:

words spoken by a character are inside speech marks
e.g. 'Let me see your passports.'

words spoken by a character are separated from the rest of the sentence by a comma, a question mark or an exclamation mark.
e.g. 'You will please stay where you are,' the lieutenant said.

with every change of speaker there is a fresh paragraph

e.g. 'Do you know anything about art?'
'Rubens,' said Catherine.
'Large and fat,' I said.
'Titian,' Catherine said.
'Titian-haired,' I said.

NB There are other rules about speech or quotation marks on pages 28–9.

14 Use the passage and the rules above to help you put paragraphs and speech marks in the following.

Henderson himself was in the garden, horticulturing a cabbage, and they asked him if he had chanced to see a singed possum that morning. What's that? What, what? said Henderson Hedgehog, and when they had repeated the question, he said, You must speak up, I'm a trifle deaf. Have you seen a singed possum? shouted Bill. I can't hear you, said Henderson. Have you seen a SINGED POSSUM? roared Bill. To be sure, said Henderson, but turnips are backward. Turnips be stewed, yelled Bill in such a tremendous voice he blew his own hat off. HAVE YOU SEEN A SINGED POSSUM? Good season for the wattle blossom, said Henderson. Well, yes, but a very poor season for carrots. A man might as well talk to a carrot as try an' get some sense out of this runt of a feller, said Bill, disgusted. Come an' see if we can't find someone that it won't bust a man's vocal cords gettin' information out of.

Writing

15 Continue the following for a page.

'Why don't you forget about the whole thing?'
The girl/boy looked straight at her/his father.
'Why should I?'

16 Write a conversation between your mother and a neighbour about yourself and what is to become of you.

17 What are the two people in the pictures (below and on page 62) saying to each other? Write the dialogue.

18 It is parents' evening at school. Your English teacher and your mother are talking about your work. Write what is said.

19 You and your family are in a car stuck in a holiday traffic jam. Write the conversation.

Talking and listening

20 Form groups of four or five.
Imagine that a spaceship from Planet HL 4953 lands in the school grounds.
You are the first earth people the occupants have ever seen.
Discuss what they might find puzzling about you and the school.
Choose one of the group to report back to the class.

Learning at home

21 Review any book you have read recently.
First, write down as a heading the title, author and publisher.
Then write a short account (not more than 200 words) of the book. Was it fact or fiction? Was it an animal or a war or a spy story? Who are the main characters?
What sort of people are the characters?
Did you enjoy the book? Why?
If you did not enjoy it then give your reasons.

22 Explain each of the following expressions in simple English.

I must warn you that he is an ugly customer.
Two can play at that game.
I think we can put her off the scent.
He who pays the piper calls the tune.
It's about time you started to pull your weight.
I'm tired of hearing you blow your own trumpet.

23 The meanings of these words are given below.
Copy out each word and write the correct meaning beside it.

glint swathe knave adze stark
weir jaunt gibe sloth buff

. . . a sneering remark
. . . a rogue, a rascal
. . . dull-yellow colour
. . . to wrap or swaddle with a bandage
. . . complete and utter, downright
. . . a dam in a stream to raise the water
. . . a hand cutting-tool, something like an axe, but with its blade at right angles to the handle.
. . . idleness, laziness
. . . to sparkle, to gleam, to glitter
. . . a short trip, a pleasant excursion

4 Explanation

This is the most common kind of writing. It is used to tell about something or to tell what it means. It is the kind of writing that explains how a thing works, or what the facts are about a subject, or why something is important. Such writing makes a subject clear and understandable. It is the language of the textbook, the encyclopaedia and the reference book.

Contents

Humpty Dumpty Explains

'You seem very clever at explaining words, Sir,' said Alice. 'Would you kindly tell me the meaning of the poem called "Jabberwocky"?'*

'Let's hear it,' said Humpty Dumpty. 'I can explain all the poems that ever were invented—and a good many that haven't been invented just yet.'

This sounded very hopeful, so Alice repeated the first verse:—

'Twas brillig, and the slithy toves
Did gyre and gimble in the wabe:
All mimsy were the borogoves,
And the mome raths outgrabe.

'That's enough to begin with,' Humpty Dumpty interrupted: 'there are plenty of hard words there. "*Brillig*" means four o'clock in the afternoon—the time when you begin *broiling* things for dinner.'

'That'll do very well,' said Alice: 'and "*slithy*"?'

'Well, "*slithy*" means "lithe and slimy". "Lithe" is the same as "active". You see it's like a portmanteau—there are two meanings packed up into one word.'

'I see it now,' Alice remarked thoughtfully: 'and what are "*toves*"?'

'Well, "*toves*" are something like badgers—they're something like lizards—and they're something like corkscrews.'

'They must be very curious-looking creatures.'

'They are that,' said Humpty Dumpty: 'also they make their nests under sundials—also they live on cheese.'

'And what's to "*gyre*" and to "*gimble*"?'

'To "*gyre*" is to go round and round like a gyroscope. To "*gimble*" is to make holes like a gimlet.'

'And "*the wabe*" is the grass-plot round a sundial, I suppose?' said Alice, surprised at her own ingenuity.

'Of course it is. It's called "*wabe*," you know, because it goes a long way before it, and a long way behind it—'

'And a long way beyond it on each side,' Alice added.

'Exactly so. Well then, "*mimsy*" is "flimsy and miserable" (there's another portmanteau for you). And a "*borogove*" is a thin shabby-looking bird with its feathers sticking out all round—something like a live mop.'

'And then "*mome raths*"?' said Alice. 'I'm afraid I'm giving you a great deal of trouble.'

'Well, a "*rath*" is a sort of green pig: but "*mome*" I'm not certain about. I think it's short for "from home"—meaning that they'd lost their way, you know.'

'And what does "*outgrabe*" mean?'

'Well, "*outgribing*" is something between bellowing and whistling, with a kind of sneeze in the middle; however you'll hear it done, maybe—down in the wood yonder—and, when you've once heard it, you'll be *quite* content. Who's been repeating all that hard stuff to you?'

'I read it in a book,' said Alice. 'But I *had* some poetry repeated to me much easier than that, by—Tweedledee, I think it was.'

'As to poetry, you know,' said Humpty Dumpty, stretching out one of his great hands, '*I* can repeat poetry as well as other folk, if it comes to that—'

'Oh, it needn't come to that!' Alice hastily said, hoping to keep him from beginning.

Lewis Carroll
Alice in Wonderland

* The poem *Jabberwocky* is on page 111.

Questions to answer

1 Why did Alice ask Humpty Dumpty to explain the poem?
2 Alice was interrupted by Humpty Dumpty after she had read the first verse. What reason did he give for doing this?
3 Why is the word *slithy* like a portmanteau?
4 What made a *tove* a curious-looking creature?
5 If you were to *gyre* and *gimble* what would you be doing?
6 Write down three pairs of words that can be used to make the portmanteau word *wabe*.
7 What would you be doing if you were *outgribing*?
8 Explain how Alice learnt the meaning of the poem.
9 Make three of your own portmanteau words.

Language—word parts

The portmanteau word (a portmanteau is a piece of luggage which opens into two equal parts) was invented by Lewis Carroll.

It is made by joining part of one word to part of another to give the sense and sound of both.

For example, CHORTLE is made from *chuckle* and *snort* to give the idea of chuckling and snorting with glee. The joining of *squire* and *parson* to make SQUARSON is another word from Carroll.

Some modern portmanteau words are ELECTROCUTE (*electric* and *execute*), MOTEL (*motorist* and *hotel*), SMOG (*smoke* and *fog*), and BENELUX (*Belgium*, *Netherlands* and *Luxembourg*).

James Joyce (see page 58) is another writer who makes portmanteau words.

10 The word portmanteau is borrowed from the French, *porter* (to carry) and *manteau* (mantle).
Over the centuries we have borrowed and adapted many words from other languages.
Here are clues to five such borrowings.
To track down the word you may need a dictionary. The first two or three letters will act as a guide.

(a) *Clue*: The Latin word for sword is GLADIUS.

Wordtrack:
(i) What do we call a man who carried a sword with which to fight in Roman arenas?
(ii) Name a certain kind of iris that has sword-shaped leaves.

(b) *Clue*: The Spartans of ancient Greece lived in LACONIA. They were a warlike people with simple habits and few words.
Wordtrack: The area in which they lived has given us a word meaning 'using few words'. What is that word?

(c) *Clue*: The Italian for a number of shots fired at the same time is TIRATA.
Wordtrack: Find a similar English word that means a blast of words is being fired at a person or persons.

(d) *Clue*: The Gaelic word for 'army' is SLUAGH and for 'shout' it is GAIRM.
Wordtrack: Put them together and we have an English word that means, not a battle cry, but a political or advertising message.

(e) *Clue*: The Old Norse word SKRYLLA means 'to scream'.
Wordtrack: There is a similar word in English that means the shrill and piercing sound made by a bagpipe. What is that word?

11 Here are 50 words we have taken from other countries. Read through them and then:
(a) make sure you can spell each one,
(b) explain the meaning of *any ten*, and
(c) place a *further* ten in sentences that show their proper use and meaning.

Russia tundra sable steppe vodka knout
Dutch yacht easel knapsack dollar
Canada caribou lumber trapper chinook
China ketchup silk mandarin kaolin joss
India dinghy shampoo yoga juggernaut bungalow
Arabia arsenal alcohol algebra alkali almanac
South America cocaine jaguar ranch tapioca cayenne
Central America tomato chilli hurricane chocolate
Germany cobalt plunder panzer waltz blitz
Italy opera piano ballerina umbrella influenza
Spain sherry bravado cockroach

12 These ten words have been borrowed from the French. For each one write down the letter of the meaning you think correct.

(i) *CHIC*
a latest fashion
b affected
c smart and stylish
d graceful

(ii) *CACHE*
a a hiding place
b cellar
c ready money
d summary

(iii) *CUL-DE-SAC*
a reception room
b acute pain
c road closed at one end
d smartly dressed person

(iv) *LIAISON*
a climbing plant or vine
b old French coin
c connection or communication between people
d optical illusion

(v) *LARGESSE*
a very large
b generous giving
c uneasiness
d extravagance

(vi) *BLASÉ*
- a gaiety
- b educated
- c trumpeted
- d bored or indifferent

(vii) *CHARLATAN*
- a imposter or fake
- b clown
- c receptacle for flowers
- d upstart

(viii) *FAÇADE*
- a triumphant shout
- b false or deceptive exterior
- c fascination
- d impudence

(ix) *RICOCHET*
- a return to sleep
- b to skip or rebound one or more times from the surface hit
- c to shatter
- d confusion

(x) *COUP*
- a unexpected or clever victory
- b blind alley
- c small shed for chicken
- d hand-to-hand fight

Listening

Ask your teacher to give the following listening tests.

13 Write and punctuate a dictation passage of about 150 words from a book you have read.
Correct spelling will be required.

14 Listen to a comprehension passage of about 400 words on which you will be asked five questions. Use the following test procedure.

- The five questions should be in front of you.
- The passage is to be read twice at normal speed.
- During the first reading do not look at the questions or write anything.
- Look at the questions when the first reading is finished.
- Wait one minute before the second reading.
- Look at the questions during the second reading.
- Write answers to the five questions.

Learning at home

15 Read the following three-sentence composition about swimming.

Swimming is a good form of exercise for people of all ages as it keeps the arms, shoulders, legs and back in a healthy condition, and makes the swimmer give his attention to deep and regular breathing. Swimming is also a sport which gives pleasure to all who practise it, whether old or young, especially when the weather is sunny. In addition, it is very refreshing to take a plunge in the hot days of summer into a cool river or outdoor swimming pool.

This composition was written by a thirteen-year-old girl. In it she tried to:

- introduce the topic of swimming
- say what was important about it
- leave out anything unimportant
- end it in a satisfactory way

To do this she:

- jotted down her ideas before writing
- made sure she could fit these ideas into three sentences

Try this exercise for yourself with a topic of your own choosing.

16 Look at the picture on page 68. Imagine you could walk into this picture. Describe all that you would see and hear.

Explaining Science

Blood pressure is measured with a sphygmomanometer (sfig-mo-mah-nom-e-ter). *Sphygos* means pulse. The pulse is the throbbing in the arteries caused by the beating of the heart. Manometer means pressure gauge.

A rubber bag is placed around the patient's left upper arm. A rubber tube inside the bag is connected with a manometer. The doctor inflates the bag like a football from a bulb in his hand. He pumps air into the bag until the pressure in the bag is greater than the blood pressure in the arteries of the arm. No blood can get past the bag so the pulse beat in the arm stops.

Then the doctor slowly lets air out of the bag. When the pressure in the bag goes down just enough to let the arteries open up so that the blood can get through, the doctor hears the pulse with his stethoscope. The reading on the manometer at the time the pulse starts again is the blood pressure.

In a thunderstorm, the noise of thunder and the light of lightning are produced at the same time. The light, however, moves through the air much faster than the noise. Light travels at 186,000 miles per second so when you see lightning you see it almost exactly as it happens. Sound is a much slower traveller and can only manage 1,128 feet per second or one fifth of a mile per second. So, unless a thunderstorm is right overhead, the sound of thunder will reach you much later than the flash of lightning.

This lag between flash and crash can be used to find out how far away a storm is, and whether or not it is coming towards you or

going away. You will need a watch with a second hand so that you can count the number of seconds between the flash of lightning and the sound of thunder that follows it. When you have this number divide it by five. For instance, if 20 seconds is counted between the two then the storm is four miles away.

Do this several times and if the distance is getting shorter the storm is coming towards you. If the distance grows longer, then the storm is passing you by or going away from you.

Questions to answer

'Blood pressure is measured . . .'

1 What is another name for a 'pulse pressure gauge'?
2 How does the manometer connect with the inflatable bag?
3 In one sentence, explain how the rubber bag is inflated.
4 At what stage does the doctor stop pumping air into the bag?
5 What stops the beat of the pulse in the left arm?
6 When is the doctor able to hear the pulse beat again?

'In a thunderstorm . . .'

7 In one sentence explain why the sound of thunder arrives after the flash of lightning.
8 When is the only time the sound of thunder does not arrive later than the flash of lightning?
9 How can the speed of light and the speed of sound be used to find out how far away a storm might be?
10 How can one judge whether or not a storm is coming nearer or going away?

Writing

11 Give a simple explanation of what a thermometer is and how it works. Use the first explanation on page 68 as a guide.
The word thermometer comes from the Greek *therme* meaning heat and *metron*, meaning a measure.
12 Write an explanation of how to play either *Hangman* or *Battleships*. Remember to give the rules in the right order.
13 Explain how you would organise a family picnic. Where would you go? What foods would you take? What equipment would you need? Tell in as much detail as possible.
14 Use the information given below to write *your* explanation of how this robbery was carried out and by whom.

On 15 May 1855, £20,000 of gold was sent from London Bridge Station to Paris by the night mail of the South Eastern Railway.

The gold, in bars, dust and coin, was packed in three boxes which were fastened by screws, double sunk into the woodwork, the holes of which were filled with wax and then officially sealed.

The boxes were placed in iron safes, secured by Chubb locks, in the guard's van. They were weighed before starting on the journey, weighed again when taken out of the safes at Folkestone, weighed a third time when landed from the steamer at Boulogne, and given a final weighing upon arrival in Paris.

The weights tallied at each place, the seals and screws were intact, yet when the boxes were opened over £12,000 had vanished and lead had taken its place.

Language—word parts: the root

A *root* is a source from which something grows.

In English a root is a word, or part of a word, from which all other forms of that word grow.

e.g. *port* is a root. From that root we get:

trans—port
port—able
trans—port—able
port—er
port—manteau

From page 65 we know that *port* comes from the French *porter* meaning 'to carry'. Thus, all the words above are connected in some way with carrying.

Knowing the root of a word is a vital guide to its meaning.

15 The root of a word may come from one of a number of languages.
Here are six roots from Greek, together with their meanings and examples.

root	*meaning*	*example*
bios	life	biography
grapho	to write	graphic
hydor	water	hydrofoil
micro	small	microscope
octo	eight	octopus
phone	sound	telephone

Use a dictionary to find and write down two other examples for each of these roots.

16 Latin roots are often used as a base for English words. Here are six, together with their meanings and examples.

root	*meaning*	*example*
aqua	water	aqualung
audio	to hear	audience
ignis	fire	ignite
scribo, scriptum	to write	describe
via	way	viaduct
video, visum	to see	visible

Use a dictionary to find and write down two other examples for each of these roots.

17 The Latin root *corpus* or *corporis* means 'body'.
Use a dictionary to find words with the following meanings.
The root gives a clue to the first few letters of the word you want to find.
(a) a dead body
(b) very fat
(c) any physical punishment
(d) a body of people permitted by law to act as a single person
(e) any of the red or white cells in the blood
(f) an organised group of ballet dancers

18 The Greek root *aer* means 'air'.
Use a dictionary to find words with the following meanings. The root gives a clue to the first few letters of the word you want to find.
(a) a small airport
(b) the air around the earth and the space beyond it
(c) the art of doing tricks in an aircraft
(d) to put air or gas into a liquid
(e) the science that studies the forces of moving air
(f) the science of the operation and flight of aircraft

Talking

19 Take turns to explain clearly to the class any one of the following. Make each explanation last for at least two minutes.
(a) make a pot of tea
(b) get from your home to the school
(c) train a dog, a horse, an elephant or any other animal
(d) direct a car into a tight parking space
(e) coax a reluctant cat down from a tree
(f) borrow money from a friend

Learning at home

20 Here are some meanings of words that have their roots in Old English.
Write out each missing word by checking the meaning and the Old English root.

e.g. to separate and drive chaff from grain (Old English *windwian* meaning 'to fan') answer: winnow

(a) to go with the wind or tide (O.E. *drifan*, to drive)
(b) a sleeping place for a baby (O.E. *cradol*, a basket)
(c) a basket made from strips of wood

and used for carrying fruit, vegetables and flowers (O.E. *trog*, boat-shaped)

(d) to leave lonely by death (O.E. *bereafian*, to rob)

(e) sour, sharp or painful (O.E. *bitan*, to bite)

21 The Anglo-Saxons liked to play word games.
Here is an example from *The Exeter Riddle Book*.
Line 8 will help you answer this riddle.

In former days my mother and father
forsook me for dead, for the fulness of life
was not yet within me. But another
woman graciously fitted me out in soft
garments, as kind to me as to her own
children, tended and took me under her
wing; until under shelter, unlike her kin,
I matured as a mighty bird (as was my
fate).
My guardian then fed me until I could fly,
and could wander more widely on my
excursions; she had the less of her own
sons and daughters by what she did thus.

Riddle No. 9
trans. Kevin Crossley-Holland

The Automatic Sheet-Changer

We walked upstairs and into a bedroom on the first floor. It was furnished in excellent Moroccan taste. I say excellent with some reservations. I personally am not too fond of that style. But aside from these observations, I noticed nothing unusual about the room at first.

'Have there been improvements made in this room?' I asked.

'Mrs M. used to be a nurse,' replied Mr F., 'and to nurses bed-making seems to become extremely boring after a while. If you stop to think of it, nurses in large hospitals spend a good deal of their time in making beds. It is natural that they should soon tire of it, particularly when they suddenly find themselves to be as rich as Mrs M. We all came to Mrs M.'s rescue with this amazing bed. It has continuous sheets.'

'How does it work?' I immediately inquired.

Mr F. walked over to Mrs M.'s bureau, opened the top drawer, and took from there a crank. He inserted the crank into a hole in the footboard of the bed and asked me to watch closely. He started to twist the crank and the sheets started to move across the bed, passing on rollers through a sideboard on through the floor.

'When I twist this crank,' explained Mr F., 'the sheets pass through this sideboard down through the floor into the cellar. There, they pass through a boiler where they are washed, then through a drying machine. They next pass through steamheated rollers where they are pressed; then come up through the floor, through the other sideboard of the bed on rollers, and back to the top of the bed. This continuous sheet is marked off in bed-widths. Every morning Mrs M. simply turns the crank until a bed width has passed from one side to the other side of her bed. This action starts the washing machines, diverts heat from the furnace to the drying machine, and while one length of sheet is being pressed, fresh widths of hot white sheets are revealed on her bed.'

'Incredible!' I exclaimed. 'But what about blankets?'

'Good Lord, man,' said Mr F., 'we never use blankets here. We're just a few miles below the Equator.'

'Oh that's right,' I said. 'Have you made inventions for every room in this house?'

William Pène du Bois
The 21 Balloons

Questions to answer

1 In one sentence for each, explain what these words mean.
You may use a dictionary if you wish.

continuous crank automatic
sideboard divert reservations

2 Why do nurses become bored with bed-making?
3 What allowed Mrs M. to escape from bed-making?
4 How were the sheets made to move across the bed?
5 Explain in one sentence what happened to the sheets in the cellar.
6 Why was the continuous sheet marked off in bed-widths?
7 What action started the washing machines every morning?
8 Why were there never any blankets on Mrs M.'s bed?
9 Make a rough drawing of this invention. Put the bed at the top of the paper, with the continuous sheet passing through the sideboard down to the cellar and back again. Place the cellar and its machinery at the bottom of the page.
10 Think of a good title for this passage.

Writing

11 'Have you made inventions for every room in this house?'
Invent something for one of the other rooms.
Explain carefully how it works.
12 Write a simple explanation of the working of any domestic appliance in your home.
13 Explain in not more than 100 words the kind of work done by each of the following.

a hairdresser
a plumber
a painter and decorator

14 Write explanations in not more than 60 words for each, of any TWO of the following:

rain snow wind lightning a rainbow
an eclipse

15 You have been sent to the Head's room for playing truant or not working properly or for misbehaving or whatever.
Write the explanation you would give.

Language—word parts: the prefix

A *prefix* is a letter or group of letters placed in front of a root word to make a new word with a different meaning.

e.g. the prefix *anti* means 'opposite' or 'against'

Place it in front of the following roots and there is a new word meaning exactly the opposite, e.g.

freeze	antifreeze
perspirant	antiperspirant
social	antisocial
cyclone	anticyclone
clockwise	anticlockwise
biotic	antibiotic

A Heath Robinson contraption for eating peas

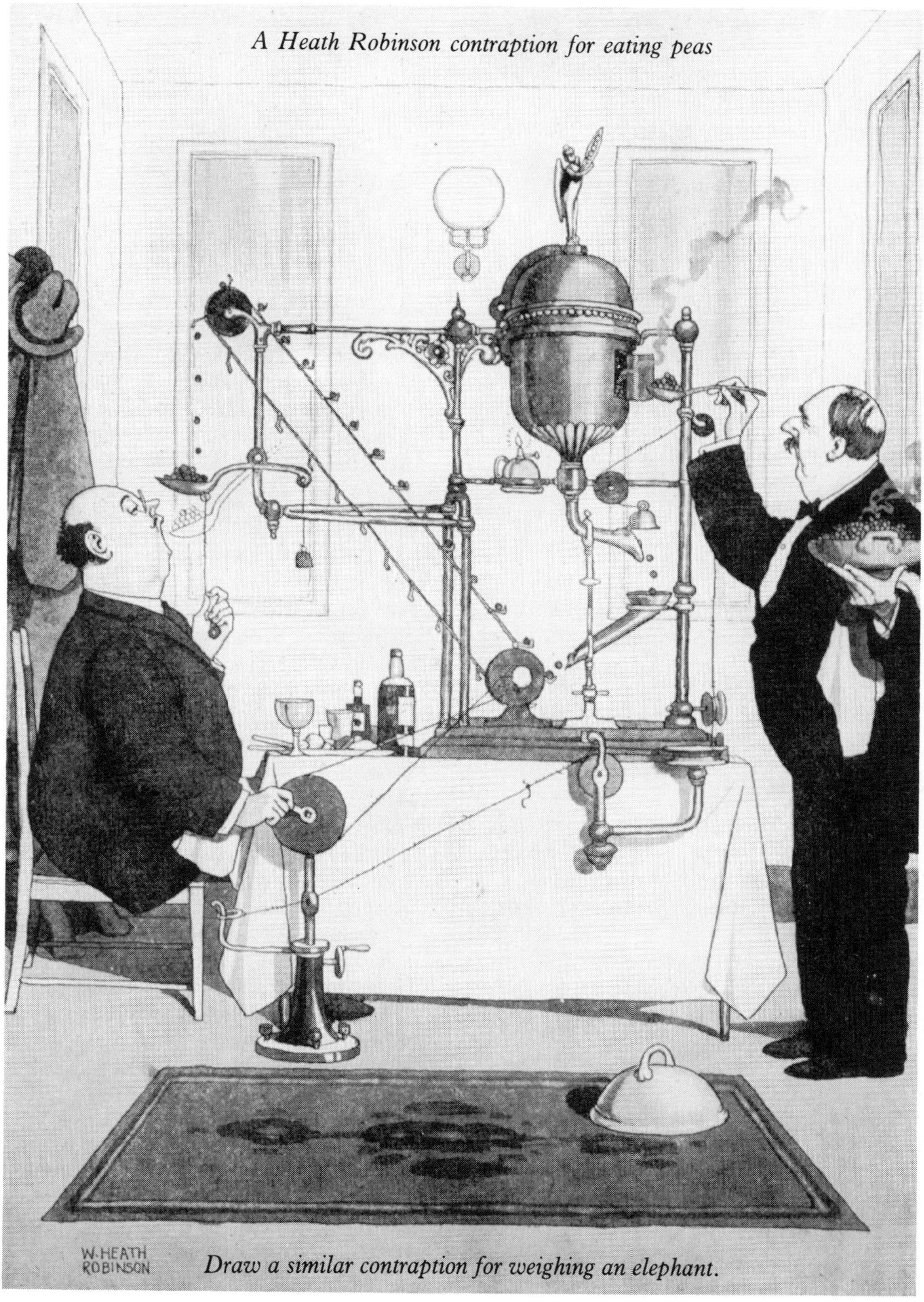

Draw a similar contraption for weighing an elephant.

16 The prefix *male, mal* or *mau* means 'badly' or 'ill' as in 'maltreat'.
Use a dictionary to find words that fit the following meanings.
The prefix gives a clue to the first few letters of the word you wish to find.
(a) a disorder or a disease
(b) badly formed or shaped
(c) bad management
(d) a person is discontented and inclined to rebel
(e) a curse
(f) a criminal or a wrongdoer
(g) an unlawful act
(h) to pretend to be ill in order to escape work

17 Here are some words that begin with the prefix *pre*. When used at the beginning of a word *pre* means 'before'.

e.g. *prehistoric* means 'before recorded history'

Work out the meanings of these words, then use each one in a sentence.

prepare predict predetermine preface
precast precaution preview prewar

Talking and listening

18 Form groups of four or five to discuss any of the following. Take turns to report your discussion to the rest of the class.
(a) School is not the only place we learn things
(b) Problems of getting to sleep
(c) What makes good television?
(d) What do you dread or fear about hospitals?
(e) Is it possible to have too much money?

Learning at home

19 This fun notice, written in fake German and English, was found pinned next to an office photocopier.
Can you translate it into plain English?

ACHTENSHUN

Das machinen is nodt for gerfingerpoken und mitten grabben. Ist ezy for brekken das Springenwerks, blowen Fusen mit loudish Popen and Spitzensparken. Ist nix gewerken by Dumkopfs! Das Rubbernekken Sighdtseeren und stupidsch Gooffoffers bast relaxen, kipp Handen in Pokkets and vatch das Stoffa kumoudt!

DAS MANICHMINDT

20 In the eighth and ninth centuries the eastern part of Britain was invaded and settled by people from Scandinavia.
The language they brought with them was called Old Norse and we remember it for the thousands of place-names in Yorkshire, Lincolnshire, Norfolk, Suffolk, Cumberland and Northumberland that end in *by, thorp* or *torp, beck, dale, thwaite* and *toft*.
Use a good map of England, or a motoring map, to study the place-names of the north-east. Write out the names of 30 places that have a Norse ending, e.g. Leesdale, Whitby and Mablethorpe.
Try to give at least one each of the endings mentioned above.
From this evidence can you say how widespread the invasion was?

Mardi Gras

Mardi Gras means 'Fat Tuesday' in French and it is the last big day of fun and feasting before the forty days of Lent. These are the fasting days during which, in earlier times, Roman Catholics stopped eating meat.

The Latin word 'carnelevarium' means to take away or remove

meat, and from this comes our word 'carnival'. In fact, carnival started in Italy many centuries ago as a Roman feast.

In England, carnival-like celebrations were held on Shrove Tuesday, the day before fasting began, right up until the nineteenth century. An early kind of football was played and this often turned into riots between rival villages. After such contests there were feasts of pancakes and much drinking.

Mardi Gras is celebrated in France with crêpes which are thin pancakes filled with sweet foods like apple sauce or cooked fruit, sprinkled with sugar. A diet like that would make any Tuesday fat! In earlier times a great ox was paraded through the streets of Paris, a copy of the Roman procession of sacrifice.

The tradition of feasting and fun is carried on in the Americas. In New Orleans, the two weeks before Mardi Gras are filled with parades, both day and night, which reach a peak on Mardi Gras with the great Rex parade. Many people dress up in costume to watch and revellers on the floats throw 'doubloons' and strings of beads to the crowds.

Mardi Gras is also celebrated in Rio de Janeiro and Trinidad. In Trinidad nearly everyone takes part either as a spectator or a reveller. Millions of dollars are spent on colourful costumes, rum-making and food. Steel bands provide music for the parades and for 'jump-up' as the dancing is called.

Carnival now has little to do with a religious feast. It is true that many Christians still give up some of their pleasures for Lent, but the pre-Lenten days now have a life of their own. It seems that once in a while people need to forget themselves, their fears and worries, in the fantasy and rhythm of carnival and Mardi Gras.

Questions to answer

1 In one sentence for each, explain the meaning, as used in the passage, of the following words:

feast fasting diet procession sacrifice reveller doubloons fantasy

2 In one sentence, explain how we obtained our word *carnival*.
3 What is the last day before the start of Lent called?
4 Name the link between a Roman feast and an early French Mardi Gras.
5 In one sentence, explain the link between the French Mardi Gras and the early English one.
6 Which is the biggest and most important of all the Mardi Gras parades in New Orleans?
7 What is the dancing called that takes place to the rhythm of a steel band during carnival in Trinidad?
8 In the writer's view, why is it that people need a modern non-religious carnival?
9 In one sentence, explain what this passage is about.

Writing

10 On page 76 there is a picture of Notting Hill Carnival. Put yourself in the place of one of the people in the picture and tell about your day.
11 Write about carnival in any way you wish. It could be a story, a poem or an article.

Language—word parts: the suffix

A *suffix* is a group of letters added to the end of a root word to alter its meaning or use. If we take the words *sudden*, *kind* and *happy* and add the suffixes *-ness* and *-ly* we change their use.

e.g. sudden sudden—ly sudden—ness
kind kind—ly kind—ness

12 Write ten words that end with the suffix *-ful*. It means either *having or causing something*, e.g. painful, or *the amount needed to fill something*, e.g. spoonful.

13 The suffixes *-ine*, *-ina*, *-ess* and *-ette* all mean 'female', e.g.

hero–ine czar–ina lion–ess
usher–ette

Can you add another six words to this list?

14 Copy out these words and underline the suffixes.
All of them begin with the letter 'l'.
Use a dictionary to write out the meaning of (a) the suffix, (b) the complete word.

gosling monologue pestilence
phrenology apologist virulent
beadle

15 Suffixes can also be used to make:

(a) *nouns*, e.g.
tender (root) tender–ness (noun)
(b) *adjectives*, e.g.
wood (root) wood–ed (adjective)
(c) *adverbs*, e.g.
quick (root) quick–ly (adverb)

Add suffixes to the following words to make nouns, adjectives and adverbs.

nouns: resist atone loyal
adjectives: imp Christ gold
adverbs: quick length other

Use each of the new words in sentences.

16 We have seen that words can be built up in the following way:

root	port
prefix + *root*	trans + port
root + *suffix*	port + able
prefix + *root* + *suffix*	trans + port + able

Copy out these stages of word building. Use them as a model to build up the following words:

honest perfect usual comfort colour normal enchant believe credible

Learning at home

17 Here are ten adjectives.
For each one write down the letter of the meaning you think correct.

(i) *CRAVEN*
a black
b cowardly
c deceitful
d nervous

(ii) *FRUGAL*
a costing little
b doubtful
c lacking humour
d greedy

(iii) *OBESE*
a generous
b brutal
c vulgar
d very fat

(iv) *FURTIVE*
a grim
b sly, stealthy
c timid, fearful
d never still

(v) *JADED*
a stingy
b abrupt
c costly
d tired out, weary

(vi) *BILINGUAL*
a speaking many languages
b very talkative
c speaking two languages
d very artistic

(vii) *VITRIOLIC*
a success in battle
b to move rapidly to and fro
c sharp and biting
d watchful

(viii) *SPECTRAL*
a someone who watches something
b a small spot, a tiny piece
c covered with specks
d ghostly

(ix) *VIBRANT*
a spiteful
b alive, powerful and exciting
c common
d to and fro movement of a stretched wire

(x) *GARISH*
a unpleasantly coloured or ornamented
b making food look and taste better
c thin cloth from India
d belonging to the stomach

18 Write out this passage putting in the words that are missing. Choose the words from this list:

ages mentioned discovered acted principal recent carrying about (twice) knows played skin oil such swinging cooking served uses butter turned

Butter was first . . . in the Bible, . . . 2150 BC (Genesis 18.8). But no-one really . . . when it was first . . . . Perhaps herdsmen found out . . . it accidentally, when they were . . . milk in goatskins. The skins . . . to and fro could have . . . as miniature churns, and . . . the milk into . . . . Through the . . . butter has been put to all sorts of . . . . It has . . . a part in ritual ceremonies, . . . as the Hindu marriage feast, and has . . . as cosmetic for the . . . and hair, a medical tonic, a salve for burns, and . . . for lamps, even as axle grease. In . . . times, the . . . uses of butter have been as a spread and in . . . .

A Guide to Butter in Britain
Butter Information Council

19 Check back on all the work you have done in this section. Write down words whose meaning you still do not know. Ask your teacher or a parent for the meaning of each word or look it up in a dictionary. Write the meaning by the side of the word. Use each of the words in a sentence to show you know its meaning.

5 Personal expression

People often dress or behave in a certain way in order to express themselves as individuals. Self expression may also be found in personal language: the kind used in speech, diaries, letters and autobiographies.

Such writing not only describes things seen and done but also reveals the author's feelings about those things. The personality shows through the writing.

A different kind of personal expression is the interest in family history. Making a family tree is now a hobby for many people and the section starts with an example of this.

Contents

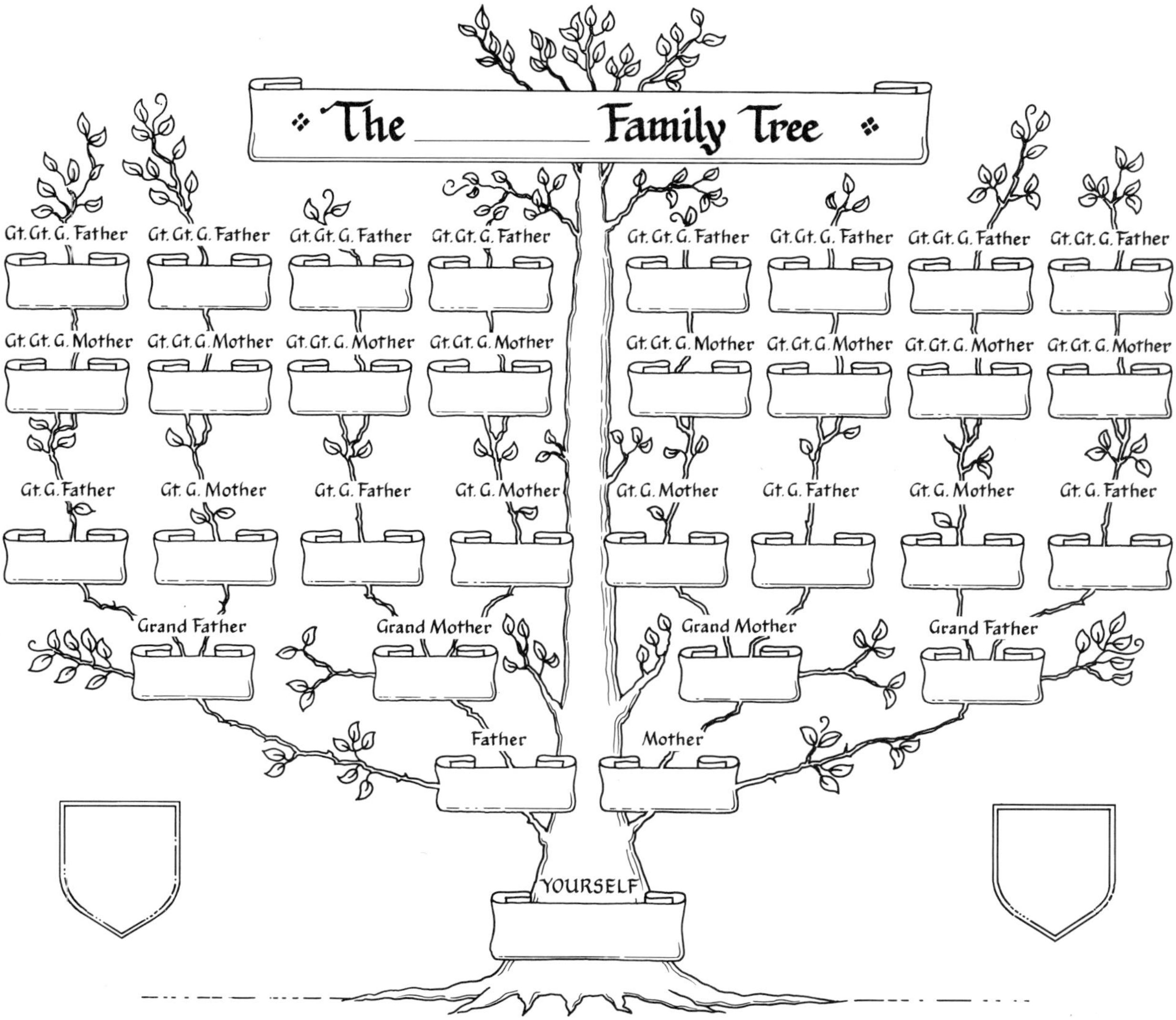

Here is some information about the Heath family together with its coat of arms.

Study both of them carefully before answering the questions.

The name Heath means 'dweller on the heath' and comes from the Olde English word *hæd*. Some early examples of the name are as follows: John de la Heth (1248); Laurence atte Hethe (1296); Peter del Heth (1297); Alan Othehethe (1332).

The arms of a Heath family is: Argent, a cross engrailed, between twelve billets gules. The Crest: a wolf's head, erased, per pale, sable and or, and ducally gorged argent, holding in his mouth a broken spear or, headed argent.

That is, a white (argent, silver) shield with a red (gules) cross made up of semicircular indents (engrailed). In the four quarters made by the cross are twelve small oblong pieces (billets) the same colour as the cross. The Crest: a wolf's head divided by a vertical line (per pale), one side of which is black (sable), the other yellow (or, gold); the wolf's neck has jagged edges, representing the neck as if torn from the body (erased). Around the neck (gorged) is a coronet of white (argent, silver), the tip of the spear is also white, and the broken shaft in the mouth of the wolf is yellow (or, gold).

Two mottoes are recorded for the name of Heath: 'Espere mieux' (Hope for better) and 'Industriae praemium' (The reward of industry).

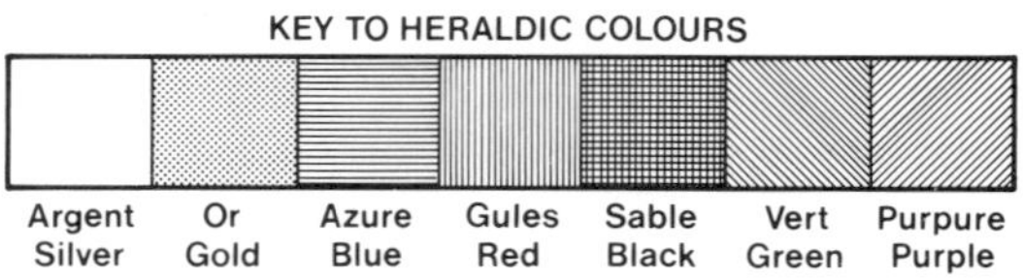

HEATH

Questions to answer

1 In which year was the name Heath or Heth first recorded?
2 From which O.E. word does the name Heath come and what is its meaning?
3 What do we now call each of these heraldic colours?

argent or azure gules sable vert purpure

4 What is meant by each of the following heraldic terms?

engrailed billets erased per pale gorged crest

5 What are the two main colours of a Heath coat of arms?
6 The crest contains a wolf's head. How is it coloured?
7 Why are there jagged edges to the wolf's neck?
8 What does the wolf carry in its mouth?
9 What is around the neck of the wolf?
10 Which of the two mottoes do you prefer? Give a reason for your choice.

Writing

11 Make a personal file telling who you are and what you are like.
Include some or all of the following:

- a description of yourself as you might appear to the rest of the class—height, build, age, clothing, shoes, colour of complexion, eyes and hair, and walk, speech and manner
- any interesting family background
- the kind of food and drink you enjoy
- what you do in your spare time
- your kind of humour
- how you feel when you are in a crowd or when punished or when chased or under water, etc.
- your views on anything you feel strongly about—gambling, smoking, drinking, homework, pocket money, etc.
- what you enjoy seeing, hearing or smelling
- what makes school hard or easy for you
- the help or guidance you need from adults
- how you get along with parents
- how you feel about growing up

12 Why is there a wolf in the crest of the Heath coat of arms? Why does that wolf have its head torn from its neck? Why is the head in two colours? Why does the wolf carry a spear with a broken shaft in its mouth? Why is there a coronet around the wolf's neck?
Make up a story that explains the presence of the wolf's head on the Heath coat of arms.
13 Make a coat of arms for yourself. First write a description as on page 79, then draw the coat of arms. You may need to do some research in the library if you attempt anything grand.

Language—vocabulary

The prefix *sur* in the word *surname* means 'over' and 'above'.

In Anglo-Saxon times most people were happy with a personal or Christian name and it was not until after the Norman Conquest that the surname was added.

These added names were usually taken from:

- the place in which the person lived
- the kind of work the person did
- some part of the body that was noticeable
- the personal name of the father

Such surnames still survive, e.g.

surnames from geographical features

Radford	red ford
Catchpole	a strip of land that is a parish boundary
Hale	a narrow valley
Stanfield	a stony field
Bradwell	a broad stream

occupational surnames

Porter	a doorkeeper
Bateman	a boatman
Fletcher	maker of bows and arrows
Wright	a man who wrought (or worked) in wood
Smith	a man who smited (or worked) in metal

surnames relating to parts of the body

Redhead	one with red hair
Brockett	badger head
Puddifoot	thick or stumpy foot
Dogett	dog's head

surnames from father's personal name
(NOTE: *O'* and *Mac* are Irish prefixes meaning 'son of'. *Fitz* means 'son of' and comes from an old French word.)

Fitzherbert	son of Herbert
O'Grady	son of Grady
MacNamara	son of Namara
Jackson	son of Jack

Use the information given above to help you answer the following questions.

14 What do you think was the work that lay behind each of the following names? A dictionary may be of help.

Tyler Brewer Mason Slater
Cartwright Skinner Thatcher
Fuller Webber Hedger

15 Which is the odd name out in each of the following lists? Say why you chose it.

(a) Johnson O'Brien Macdonald Cooper
(b) Goldsmith Robson Bowyer Fletcher
(c) Wainwright Dale Heath Townsend
(d) Hardwick Lightfoot Whale-belly Whitehead

16 Explain how *Townsend* could be not only a name but also an address.
17 Find as many occupational surnames as you can. A telephone directory or a biographical dictionary might be useful.
18 Most occupational surnames come from previous centuries. Invent six new surnames that relate to work in the twentieth century, e.g.

Peter Doctorson Jane MacArchitect
Mary Marine John Pilot Ian
O'Warden Anita Dentist

19 Here is a list of personal names that mean *John* in other languages.
Can you say to which country each belongs?

Giovanni Ivan Sean Juan
Jan Hans Evan Ian

Learning at home

20 Here are ten words relating to families. For each one write down the letter of the meaning you think correct.

(i) *PATRIARCH*
a a person who loves his country
b one of the governing class in ancient Rome
c a person who murders his father
d a man who leads a family

(ii) *KIN*
a a person's pedigree
b male descendants
c a person's relatives
d a bantling

(iii) *CLAN*
a a tribe
b a secret society
c a group of like-minded people
d a large family forming a close group

(iv) *SIRE*
a a descendant
b an uncle by marriage
c a father or male ancestor
d a half-brother

(v) *MATRICIDE*
a a family of numbers
b the crime of killing one's mother
c a woman who leads a family
d a female godparent

(vi) *POLYGAMY*
- a marriage to more than one wife at a time
- b a belief that there is only one god
- c one of a family of light plastic materials
- d marriage to one person at a time

(vii) *SCION*
- a a minor prince
- b a family black sheep
- c a young member of a family
- d the weakest member of a family

(viii) *PROGENY*
- a related by blood
- b a favourite son
- c a distant relation
- d offspring or descendants

(ix) *FORBEARS*
- a guardians
- b country cousins
- c ancestors
- d counsellors

(x) *SIBLING*
- a a woman from the ancient world
- b one of a pair of twins joined together since birth
- c a brother or sister
- d an evil-tempered mother

21 Copy the family tree on page 79, or ask your teacher to run off copies for the class.
First, fill in your own name and your date of birth. Follow this with the same details for your mother and father.
Get the same information from your grandparents. Your mother and father may be able to help if your grandparents do not live near you.
Your grandparents, should they be still living, may then be able to give the names and dates of birth of your great-grand-parents.

22 Suppose you now want to go back beyond your great-grandparents.
Since 1837 it has been the law that all births, marriages and deaths should be listed at St Catherine's House in London. Try to make a visit and get more details about your family tree.

The Coble Landing

Another favourite excursion was to the 'Coble Landing', which, if I recall it right, was at the very ending of that always endless-seeming, desolate street, Mile End Road. 'Coble' is the Geordie word for a small rowing boat, and here I suppose the coble landing was where the fishermen and tugboat men and pilots landed their craft. I don't ever remember seeing anyone land there: all that remains in my memory is a long steep flight of rickety, black, wet wooden steps that led down a precipitous bank to the River Tyne. As a child I thought it a terrible drop—there was a loose wooden railing at the edge; but heights always filled me with a kind of happy terror, and I would rock on the wooden railing and imagine myself falling, falling, falling . . .

Beyond the landing lay the great, grey river, moving slowly down into the broad harbour, bearing coasters, pilot-craft, tugs, trawlers, dredgers, ferry boats, oil tankers, and cargo ships and occasionally mournfully-hooting liners from Scandinavia. Forests of scaffolding

Write a description of this scene at Newcastle upon Tyne in 1928.

and masts rose from the shipyards, where even in daytime you could catch sight of the blue spark of a far-off acetylene burner used by an unseen welder or riveter. Those flashes were our kingfishers. It was the same sort of blue flash as that made by our tram-trolleys.

James Kirkup
The Only Child

Questions to answer

1 Look up the following words in a dictionary. Write out each one with the meaning by its side.

excursion desolate rickety
precipitous acetylene

2 Where was the 'Coble Landing'?
3 Why was it called the 'Coble Landing'?
4 Explain where the flight of wooden steps led.
5 What did the child's 'happy terror' lead him to imagine?
6 Where did the 'great, grey river' move to?
7 What evidence is there that the river is deep?
8 Explain in your own words the kind of sound made by the hooters of the Scandinavian liners.
9 Why are the scaffolding and masts described as 'forests'?
10 The blue sparks of an acetylene burner are described as kingfishers. In your own words explain why.

Writing

11 Write about an early childhood experience which made an impression on you.

12 Read the extract in question 15. Write your own story about robots. It might be called *The Robots Strike Back* or *The March of the Robots.*

13 Imagine you have spent a weekend in the home of a friend. Write a thank you letter to his or her mother.

14 Write about anything you have made either at home or in school.

Language—tense

The word *tense* comes from the Latin *tempus* meaning 'time'.

Hence, the tense of a verb tells us *when* an action takes place.

In English there are three simple tenses:

present	I take
past	I took
future	I shall take

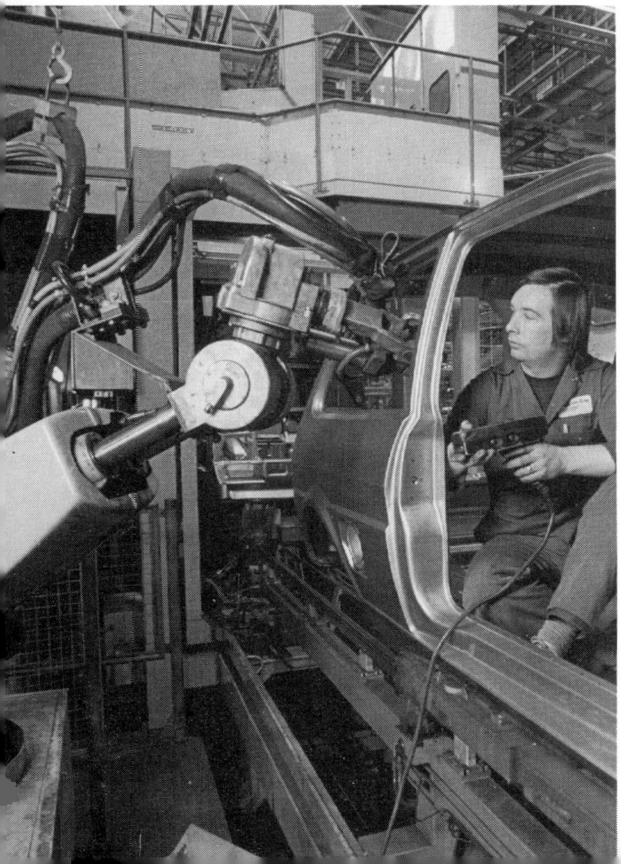

Writing in the past tense is easy. One simply writes about something that has happened. It might have happened:

this morning
yesterday
last week
a month ago
last year
ten years ago
centuries ago

It doesn't matter when so long as it happened in the past.

15 Read the following and then say in which of the three tenses it is written.

A maintenance worker in a Tokyo car factory was killed when a robot suddenly started up, struck him in the back, and then pinned him against another machine. It was Japan's first recorded death in an accident involving an industrial robot. An inquiry said that the victim was guilty of carelessness but that the safety measures on the robot were not adequate.

16 Charles Dickens wrote this story in the present tense. Write it out in the past tense.

The Cricketer
The tall thin man who is sitting near the rather plump gentleman with spectacles is interrupting those who are watching the cricket match. The plump gentleman politely asks him whether he plays cricket. The tall thin stranger says he does. 'It is in the West Indies,' he says. 'We play all afternoon in the boiling hot sun. My side makes 670 runs. Then we go in to field. The other side makes 660 after hours of batting in the heat of the sun which glows like a furnace. Then Colonel Blazo comes in to bat. He must not get those ten runs. The heat is terrific. The captain puts me on to bowl. Blazo has to be got out. He hits my first ball. He runs two runs. So great is the heat, Colonel Blazo almost collapses. But he is determined to stay in. I bowl again. Feebly Blazo lifts his bat. It is

scorched to a cinder in the blazing heat. "No ball," cries the umpire, as the ball I bowl bursts into flames. A new ball and a new bat are called for. This is the last over. It is so hot we can scarcely stagger about the field. I bowl again. Blazo hits it for six and his servants run on the field and throw iced water over him. He revives at once. He has two to make to equal our score. I stagger up to bowl. Blazo misses. There are three more balls in the over. Can I endure it? With trembling fingers I pick up the scorching ball and polish it on my trousers. It burns a hole in them as big as a frying pan. I bowl. Blazo makes one supreme effort and hits the ball back to me along the ground. The grass gives off clouds of smoke as the ball rolls over it. I bowl the last ball but one. Two men are now holding Blazo up. But it is all over. Blazo can do nothing except give a weak flick of his bat. The last ball is bowled. I hit the wickets. The last ball bowls Blazo out.' 'Extraordinary,' says the plump gentleman.

Listening

17 Organise a class discussion about the importance of listening. The following may give you some ideas.

- why do we want others to listen to us?
- what part does listening play in conversation?
- how does listening affect speaking?
- how does listening affect school work?
- what can hinder listening?

18 Form groups of four or five.
Discuss the fact that one cannot listen properly if there are distractions.
Think about distractions within the last fortnight in such situations as:

- school or year assemblies
- the classroom
- school work at home
- listening to radio or TV

List these distractions and try to add one way to overcome each one.
Choose a group member to report back to the class.

19 Form groups of four or five.
How well does each member listen in discussion?
Does he or she:

- look directly at the speaker
- show the speaker interest
- ask questions which help the speaker make his meaning clear
- attend to the main points of the discussion
- bring the conversation back to the point if it begins to ramble
- disagree with the speaker in a polite and courteous way
- think so hard about what they are going to say that they do not listen to others

After discussion, list all the above on a sheet of paper.
By *group decision* give a mark out of ten to each member for performance in these areas.

Learning at home

20 Imagine you were in Ford's Theatre on the evening of 14 April 1865.
Describe the following incident *as it happens*. You can best do this by thinking of yourself as a reporter for radio.

President Lincoln, his wife, and two friends, were in the presidential box at Ford's Theatre in Washington watching a play called 'Our American Cousin'. It was the evening of the 14 April 1865. A few minutes after ten o'clock the door of the box was opened quietly and John Wilkes Booth entered. This well-known actor carried a one-shot brass derringer in his right hand. He pulled the trigger and a lead ball crashed into the left side of the President's head and lodged behind the left eye. Booth then tried to jump down to the stage but fell and broke his leg when his spur caught in a flag draped in front of the box. He limped across the stage waving a dagger and shouted the motto of Virginia—*Sic semper tyrannis*—(Thus ever to tyrants). He escaped into an alleyway and to his horse. Lincoln was carried from the theatre to a house on the opposite side of the street where he died the next morning.

Pages from Diaries

April 22

Went to Bickleigh Vale,—a deep narrow combe, running down out of the moor, with steep, wooded slopes on either side, and deep down at the bottom the river Plym winding its way. The ground was carpeted with Anemones and Blue-bells and here and there Primroses, and the tall handsome plants of the Wood Spurge were very conspicuous with their red stalks and pale green flowers. It was the first time I had ever

seen this plant. In one little open glade we came upon a bush of golden Broom flower. The vale was thickly wooded from end to end—a paradise for birds: among their notes those of the Great Tit, Chiff-chaff, Robin and Wren were specially conspicuous. We found beds of the Hairy Bitter Cress and a few blooms of the Mountain Speedwell. We walked four miles through the woods to Plym Bridge at the far end of the Vale. A Water Ouzel skimmed across the river and in under the archway of the old, grey, stone bridge, every cranny of which was green with tiny ferns. Then on to Marsh Mills Station, through narrow Devonshire lanes with high banks hanging with last year's fronds of Hart's tongue and Hard ferns. Here we found the Shining Crane's-bill, Herb Robert; Ivy-leaved Toadflax; and Treacle-Mustard in flower. After more than three weeks drought had a heavy fall of rain at night.

Edith Holden
The Country Diary of an Edwardian Lady

Thursday 15th April

. . . When we were in the woods beyond Gowbarrow park we saw a few daffodils close to the water side. We fancied that the lake had floated the seeds ashore and that the little colony had so sprung up. But as we went along there were more and yet more and at last under the boughs of the trees, we saw that there was a long belt of them along the shore, about the breadth of a turnpike road. I never saw daffodils so beautiful they grew among the mossy stones about and about them, some rested their heads on these stones as on a pillow for weariness and the rest tossed and reeled and danced and seemed as if they verily laughed with the wind that blew upon them over the lake, they looked so gay ever glancing ever changing . . . There was here and there a little knot and a few stragglers a few yards higher up, but they were so few as not to disturb the simplicity and unity and life of that one busy highway. We rested again and again.

Dorothy Wordsworth
The Grasmere Journals 1802

Questions to answer

Find answers to the following questions in the two passages on pages 87 and 88.

1 Write out the meaning of each of the following words. You may use a dictionary.

combe	conspicuous	cranny
fronds	colony	turnpike
stragglers	unity	

2 Name the river that flowed through the bottom of Bickleigh Vale.

3 What probable reason did the Wordsworths give themselves for the first few daffodils growing close to the water side?

4 Why was Bickleigh Vale a paradise for birds?

5 Of what material was Plym Bridge built?

6 What made the Wordsworths believe finally that the daffodils were planted by man?

7 What had actually happened to those daffodils described as resting their heads on the stones 'as on a pillow for weariness'?

8 What is Treacle-Mustard?

9 What colour are the flowers of the Wood Spurge?
10 To what did Dorothy Wordsworth liken the movement of the daffodils?
11 How did the belt of daffodils begin and end?
12 How do we know that a railway ran through the Bickleigh Vale area?
13 What is a Water Ouzel?
14 Dorothy Wordsworth writes about a 'busy highway'. What was that busy highway?

Writing

15 Write a page for a country diary similar to either of those on pages 87–88.
Parks, playing fields, gardens, churchyards and waste land are good places to observe wildlife should you not live in the country.

16 Use any of the following information about a village and its people to help you write a story.

NETHER ABBAS: population 460; village in the hills; farming area; inn, *The Crown*; church, *All Saints*; restaurant, *The Green Plunge*; Tonkin's Garage; post office; village store.
Vicar at All Saints, Reverend John Stallwood
Doctor, David Hill, M.B.
Landlord at *The Crown*, Thomas Bolton
His wife, Sue
Their son Terry, 14, at Rutherglan Comprehensive
Barmaid at *The Crown*, Bridget, 24
Postmaster, Tim Aubrey
Police Sergeant, County Constabulary, Albert Moore
His wife, Elizabeth
Their daughter, Joanne, 13, at school with Terry
Local farmer, Raymond Kennedy

17 Here are some notes on a bird called the lapwing or peewit.
Weave some of them into a diary entry of 200 words about a walk in the country in which you saw a flock of lapwing.

The Lapwing or Peewit

Recognition: 12 in. (30 cm) long; from distance looks black and white, can look brilliant green in sunshine, rounded wings, short tail, long legs, distinctive crest; in winter seen in large numbers on arable and grass farmland and on moorland; may join waders on fresh-water margins and mud-flats along coast.

Food: eats harmful insects—wire-worms, leather jackets, snails and harmful larvae; stamps feet to bring up earth-worms; useful bird, friend of farmer.

Call: bird gets both names from sounds it makes; wings make a 'lapping' sound in flight, whilst song is 'p'weet, p'weet, peewit, peewit' plus long whistling note.

Nest: scrapes in ground made by male rocking forward on breast, lined by female with dried grass; sometimes small depression in ground in field or pasture.

Eggs: olive-buff or olive-green marked with black or brown; 4; usually lays late March–May; incubation about 27 days; nests robbed by gourmets as eggs considered great delicacy.

Language—present tense

Writing in the present tense is a little more difficult than writing in the past tense (see page 85).

In the present tense one writes about something that is actually happening at that moment.

There is an example by Charles Dickens on page 85.

The tall thin man tells his story in the present tense to take us through that unbelievable cricket match in the West Indies.

We follow with interest as both bat and ball burst into flames because of the heat and the match itself is decided by the last ball.

Writing in the present tense gives the reader an experience as it actually happens.

18 Write two short pieces about any job done by someone you know.
Firstly, describe the job and how it is done.
Secondly, imagine you are that person and describe the job as you are doing it.

19 Imagine you are watching a cat stalk a bird in the garden.
Describe each movement as it actually happens.

Cockney Childhood

Petticoat Lane. I can never forget it. The sounds of the market place, the cries of the street traders and the bustle of the crowds always makes me think of my boyhood.

I was born in Holborn in the City of London. You could call me a real cockney because I was born within the sound of Bow Bells. In fact, Holborn is also within sight of Bow Bells.

My father was a working man. My mother used to do all her shopping in the Lane and all my clothes came from there, second-hand, of course. You could get anything in the Lane from a pin to an elephant.

We were very poor, so we couldn't afford an elephant, apart from which we had nowhere to keep it.

Club Row is another street I shall never forget. That's where they sold dogs and cats and rabbits. For two bob you could buy a lovely homing pigeon that flew straight back to the fellow who sold it to you. In Petticoat Lane they sold chickens, and not far from where I lived was the slaughter house where they used to kill and pluck the chickens. I can't forget the awful smell from that place.

Among many other interesting and historic street names were Frying Pan Alley, Cock Hill. My school was in Frying Pan Alley, and Cock Hill was a little square at the back where there used to be a cock-pit in the old days when they used to have cock-fighting, and we used to have our fights there.

I remember that I was pretty tall for my age, and I must admit I was a bit of a bully and liked to throw my weight around. But underneath I was a coward. If I picked a fight it was with somebody smaller than I was. I was no fool. But one time I made a mistake. He was only a little guy, but he said something to me in front of a girl and made me look a right fool. 'Right,' says I. 'See you up Cock Hill.' So there we went after school, and we drew quite a crowd, many of them girls.

They made a space for us, and we took off our jackets and set to. It must have been a silly sight because I was much bigger than he was. And there I was dancing round this little fellow like Mohammed Ali, shuffling, ducking, feinting, and not throwing one blow. He just stood still and looked at me as if I was a raving idiot. He let me carry on until I was out of breath, and then he drew back his fist, threw one punch and knocked me down.

I was out cold for about ten minutes. I could certainly pick them because that little guy grew up to become Fly-Weight Champion of the British Empire, would you believe?

Well, after that hiding, I never picked a fight with anyone ever again—big or small. I wouldn't even pick a fight with a girl. I can never forget Frying Pan Alley or Cock Hill—the marks are still on my chin.

Alfred Marks
Next Move

Questions to answer

1 What is a street trader?
2 Where must one be born in order to be a true cockney?
3 Why did the parents not buy an elephant?
4 What was sold in Club Row apart from dogs and cats?
5 How did Cock Hill get its name?
6 What made the writer think he was a coward?
7 Why did the writer's opponent look at him as if he were 'a raving idiot'?
8 Explain in your own words how the writer made a mistake in picking this fight.
9 Why was it not wise to buy a pigeon in Club Row?
10 Make up a good title for this passage.

Writing

11 Write as much as you can about a time when you were very young.

12 If you were to run a market stall what would you sell and why?

13 One wet day, you and a friend visit an old mill. No one has lived there for years. You creep quietly up a rickety old staircase. The cobwebs float against your faces in the dark. Suddenly you hear a strange noise . . .
Continue this story for another 300 words or so.

14 Write an interesting description of the area in which you live for a friend in America who has never visited this country.

15 Imagine you took part in the Second World War as a nurse, ambulance driver, air-raid warden, soldier, sailor or airman. Around you are gathered your grandchildren. Tell them the narrowest escape from death you ever had.

Language—the future tense

So far in this section we have thought about actions which either have taken place in the past or are taking place in the present.

Actions can also take place in the future.

The future of tomorrow, next week, next month, next year or the year 2005.

e.g. I visited the Kennedy Space Centre last week (past tense)
I am visiting the Kennedy Space Centre (present tense)
I shall visit the Kennedy Space Centre next year (future tense)
I shall leave the Kennedy Space Centre for my Moon holiday on 19 August 2005 (future tense)

Here is mother anticipating what will happen when you arrive at the Space Centre for that holiday:

We shall arrive in Florida at 11 a.m. on 18 August 2005 having travelled from Britain that morning by Boeing SST. I shall go to the hotel to rest after the flight. It will be an overnight stay, for the shuttle will leave at 13.20 the following day. Charles will want to explore the Centre and Angela will certainly be window-shopping in the city.

Notice the use of *shall* and *will* in the above.

It is almost impossible to write in the future tense without these two words.

When writing in the future tense some people are not sure which word to use and when. Learn the following rules and there will be no problem.

(a) use *shall* with *I* and *we*
e.g. *We shall* arrive in Florida . . .
I shall go to the hotel . . .

(b) use *will* in all other cases
e.g. *Charles will* want to explore . . .
It will be an overnight stay . . .

16 Use the information above to help you write out the following sentences and place either *shall* or *will* in each space.

(a) Melanie . . . ride a shuttle mission some time next year.
(b) A space telescope . . . be several times more powerful than any earth telescope.
(c) I . . . be thrilled to watch the take-off.
(d) The Americans . . . be building a moon base by the year 2000.
(e) There is no doubt that I . . . be carrying out experiments in space.
(f) . . . we see an astronaut, powered by a backpack, working in space?
(g) . . . John be in the shuttle with us?

Shall and *will* are also used to show determination, threat and promise.
Look at these two sentences:

Tomorrow *I shall* go to the Space Centre.
Tomorrow *I will* go to the Space Centre.

I shall go means that you intend going to the Space Centre but may change your mind.
I will go means that you are determined to go to the Centre and nothing will stop you.
The rules here are:

use *will* with *I* and *we*
use *shall* in all other cases

17 Explain the difference in meaning between the two sentences in each of the following pairs.
   (a) We shall be working on the Star Wars programme for the next twenty years.
   We will be working on the Star Wars programme for the next twenty years.
   (b) Technicians shall work overtime tonight to get the space shuttle ready.
   Technicians will work overtime tonight to get the space shuttle ready.
   (c) I will go to the launch site by myself.
   I shall go to the launch site by myself.
18 Which is the stronger of these two?

   'They shall not pass'
   'They will not pass'

   Give a reason for your choice.
19 Use the future tense to write a short story called 'When I am on holiday on the moon'.

Finally, do not mix your tenses when writing. If you begin a piece in the past tense then go on with it in the past tense. The same applies to the present tense and the future tense.

Talking and listening

20 *Class discussion:*
   (a) Do you agree with the hunting of hare, fox, deer, otter, etc., purely for sport? Do you think the hunting of wild animals should be forbidden?
   (b) Is a boarding school better for children than a day school?

Learning at home

21 A neighbour owns a savage dog which is not kept under proper control. Write a polite letter of complaint to the owner.
22 Write a letter to a neighbour *explaining* and *apologising* for an accidental breakage of his or her greenhouse roof.
23 If you were able to travel into the past or future, where would you go? Imagine a visit to another period of time and describe your experiences and the people you meet.
24 Write an account of the best kind of evening spent at home.

Tell the story of the family in this picture.

6 Argument

Language for argument tries to make the reader think or act as the writer wants him to. It may try to change a person's mind by using argument that appeals to his reason, to his emotions, or to both.

Argument that appeals to the reason tries to convince: argument that appeals to the emotions aims to persuade.

Contents

Letters to the Editor

29 Landsdowne Drive,
RADLETH,
Adalshire.

26h May

The Editor
Radleth Free Press,
Radleth,
Adalshire.

Sir,

May I complain about the way pavements are being used nowadays? I thought that pavements were for people to walk on but I find it more and more difficult to do so.

On the way home from the bus stop this morning I met on the pavement boys on bicycles, smaller children on tricycles, girls and boys on roller skates, four girls skipping, one parked car and another parked car which was being cleaned.

For an elderly person like myself these activities are worrying and dangerous. In addition, the parking of cars on pavements is illegal. Are people now so selfish that they have no concern for anyone but themselves?

I would like to make pavements safe to walk on again and readers who agree with me should write to the address above.

Yours faithfully,

William Turner
Hon. Secretary,
Pavements for Pedestrians Campaign

---

33 Cambridge Road,
RADLETH,
Adalshire.

24th May

The Editor,
Radleth Free Press,
RADLETH,
Adalshire.

Sir,

There is not much money for education these days and I would like to suggest a way in which more of it can be directed to the classroom where it is needed.

Why not introduce the European school day? There is no reason why pupils cannot start their lessons earlier each day and finish at lunch time. A lot of money would then be saved by ending the costly school meals service. This money could then be used for books and equipment needed by the teacher.

With afternoons free the older pupils would be able to do part-time work and thus put money into their pockets. The move might even cut down the truancy we hear so much about.

Teachers might also benefit. They would be free to undertake better paid work in the afternoons and thus reduce the huge bill for teachers' salaries.

I would be interested to hear the views of others on this subject.

Yours faithfully,

Nicola Westbrook

Questions to answer

Find answers to the following questions in the two letters on page 95.
Write your answers in complete sentences.

1 What is a European school day?
2 Explain in your own words the real reason for having pavements.
3 Why are old people worried by activities on pavements?
4 Is it true that more money is needed in the classroom? Give your viewpoint and reasons for it.
5 What might pupils do about lunch if they could not have it at school?
6 Is it likely that teachers would take a second job in the afternoons? Give reasons for your opinion.
7 What is your view on the way pavements are used?
8 What is your view on the European school day?
9 Suggest one or two ways in which pavements might be safeguarded for pedestrians.
10 Which is the better letter? Give reasons for your choice.

Language—viewpoints

All of us have our own views and opinions about things that happen to us or things we hear about.

Sometimes in school we are asked to tell about these either in writing or discussion.

This is a useful thing to do as it helps us arrange our thoughts in an orderly way and then express them clearly.

It also makes us think again about the ideas we hold already.

When you are asked to express a viewpoint in writing make sure it is planned first.

A good way to do this is to divide a sheet of paper into two columns and in these set up all the arguments for and against the topic under discussion. For example:

ALL SCHOOLS SHOULD HAVE SOME FORM OF UNIFORM

For	*Against*
makes life simple for parents	uniform costs more
helps build a school spirit	puts children on the same level as traffic wardens, soldiers and prisoners
is an answer to untidiness by boys and overdressing by girls	if school uniform is so important why is it not worn by teachers
does away with problem of deciding what clothing to ban and what to allow	takes away personal identity
makes all pupils equal whether they come from rich or poor homes	does not allow personal taste to develop

It is now easy to make a simple plan for the essays.

e.g. para. 1 introduction
para. 2 argument for (1)
para. 3 argument for (2)
para. 4 argument against (1)
para. 5 argument against (2)
para. 6 my opinions and viewpoint

Two final points. Introduce the argument in an interesting way. Get your reader's attention in the first sentence and then tempt him or her to read on.

In your summing up in para. 6 do not forget to argue against the viewpoints you have rejected.

11 Make a *for* and *against* plan for the following topic:

'It is better to live in the country than the town'

12 For each of the following give two reasons why:
(a) Britain is the best country in the world in which to live.
(b) August is the best month for a holiday.
(c) the life of a farmer is better than the life of a shopkeeper.
(d) gambling is not a good thing.
(e) Britain is not the best country in the world in which to live.
(f) it is not a good thing to be an eldest child.
(g) you disapprove of alcohol.

13 The following was said in a talk to the parents of some young children.

Who will be better remembered — the parent who slouches in front of the television for three hours every night, or the parent who finds the time in a busy working day to find ten or fifteen minutes to read to the children. In the long run children will never remember all the television shows you watch together — but they'll always remember that together you chased monsters with Maurice Sendak or mourned the death of a friend in 'Charlotte's Web', or laughed aloud with Roald Dahl — and best of all you did it together.

Imagine you are a parent who likes to slouch in front of the television set. Write an answer to this point of view.

Writing

14 You may have visited a zoo where wild animals are kept in pits and cages. Should wild animals be kept in captivity in this way? What can be said for and against it?
15 What can be said for and against camping as a way of spending a summer holiday?
16 What can be said for and against the invention of the aeroplane?
17 Write a letter to the editor of the *Radleth Free Press* on an issue you feel strongly about. For example, you may want to Save the Whale, Plant a Tree, Adopt a Granny or Ban the Bomb. Explain your views on the issue and give the reasons for them. Use the same layout as that on page 96.

Talking

18 Give a short talk on one of the following. Collect information you think will be interesting and arrange this in an orderly way.

water divining witchcraft
haunted houses monsters of the deep
astrology vampires

Learning at home

19 Which is your favourite sport? What can be said for and against it?
20 Write down two words to show the use of each of the following prefixes.
Against each word write its meaning.

con- re- sub- trans- un-

Viewpoint

When I try to describe those thoughtless individuals who gain pleasure from using air guns to shoot at anything living and moving, the only words that come to mind cannot be used in a family magazine.

The Society of Practising Veterinary Surgeons found that 94 per cent of practices saw animals injured by air guns and 41 per cent met at least five such cases each year. There are more than 1,600 practices in the United Kingdom, so this means that we know of about 7,000 injured animals. How many others are shot and die quickly, or after days, because the wounds have become gangrenous, or how many wild animals starve when they are disabled and cannot find food, we will never know.

The Royal Society for the Protection of Birds receive reports of up to 500 incidents of wanton shooting of wild birds each year—and what they hear about can be only a tiny proportion. All of this is stupid, deliberate cruelty, and illegal.

The sale of air-gun pellets is measured in hundreds of millions. Apologists talk about 'vermin control' and target shooting. No doubt some ammunition is properly used for these purposes, but I wonder how long it is before the 15-year-old, living on an urban estate with a pocket handkerchief garden, finds that shooting at coloured paper circles is boring, and that sparrows are more exciting targets. And if next door's cat scares the birds away, he is bigger, easier to hit and so fair game, too.

As the law stands, a 15-year-old cannot legally buy an air weapon—but he can receive one as a gift. He breaks the law if he shoots at any bird or animal unless he is authorised under the Wildlife and Countryside Act, and if he is on or within 50 feet of the public highway, there is another offence. With little or no perjury, a juvenile can buy an air rifle by mail order—I don't think anyone wants to know his age. Being able to find the money is all that is required. The law is supposed to prevent the misuse of air weapons, but all the evidence suggests that the law is rarely enforced.

The number of animals shot seems to increase each year. Children are victims, too. Many organisations have appealed for a change in the law, feeling that the present laws are not being enforced and that some system of licensing holders of air weapons is essential. The Cat's Protection League collected more than a million signatures to a petition presented to Parliament but very little has happened.

To be fair, the Home Office did organise a campaign to try to educate people in the proper use of these guns. Did you notice it? There was a leaflet available, on request from police stations, but most of the hooligans who get their kicks by shooting children, cats or birds would only enter such premises as an involuntary visitor. There is no real prospect of changing attitudes in this way.

So what is my message? Think a dozen times first, and then *don't* give your favourite nephew an air gun. Be prepared to report any misuse that you might see and perhaps ask your MP what he thinks about it. Finally, I'd say to the very committed animal welfare groups, why not put some of your effects into air gun control? More than 7,000 animals would be grateful.

Woman's Realm

Questions to answer

1 (a) Write out the meaning of each of the following words, then
(b) use each word in a sentence of your own

gangrenous veterinary vermin
apologist disabled wanton
urban juvenile perjury
involuntary

2 How do we know that 7,000 animals are injured by air guns each year?
3 What makes the writer think that the figure for the number of animals injured each year may well be higher than 7,000?
4 Name two animal welfare groups mentioned in the passage.
5 Can you suggest a reason why there should be fewer birds than animals shot?
6 Is it legal for a fifteen-year-old to own an air gun?
7 Name two ways a fifteen-year-old can break the law with an air gun.
8 For what purpose did the Cat's Protection League collect more than a million signatures?
9 Why was the Home Office campaign a failure?
10 To which two groups of people is the writer sending his message?
11 Give the passage a suitable title.

Writing

12 Put yourself in the place of a pet cat or dog. Tell the story of your life near a neighbour with an air gun.
13 Study this advertisement. Give your opinion on the slaughtering of animals for their skins. Why does it need to happen? Is there a real alternative fur for women who think the wearing of furs is exciting and glamorous? Does a fur look best on the animal for which it was originally intended?

Sighting Of Rare Leopard Angers Wildlife Supporters

The sight of a leopard in the wild is one to stir the blood. Unhappily, it's a sight that is fast becoming rare. The main reason why the leopard, the elephant and the gorilla are now endangered species is because too many hunters have them in their sights: rare leopards are being slaughtered for their skins.

The World Wildlife Fund desperately needs your support in its efforts to prevent trade in endangered species. Trade in skins, ivory, even live animals, has brought many species to the verge of extinction. It's not just the leopard — over 1,000 different kinds of animals are under threat **right now**. Among them are the elephant, the rhino and the polar bear.

Please help us to save the leopard and other threatened species.

WWF U.K.
Registered charity No. 201707

14 Read several times the poem *My Mother Saw a Dancing Bear* on page 125.
Is it shameful or even cruel to make animals learn tricks in circuses to amuse the public? How do *you* feel about wild animals being kept in captivity in order to perform for humans?
Write a story or a poem that comes from your thoughts about *My Mother Saw a Dancing Bear*.

15 Write a clear description of the scene below.

Language—singular and plural : verbs

Verbs also have a singular and plural form. Look at the following.

singular	*plural*
The girl *reads* her book.	The girls *read* their books.

Note that the verb changes from *reads* to *read* when the subject is made plural.
Note also that to form the plural of most verbs the letter *s* is taken away, e.g. *reads* (singular) and *read* (plural).

16 Choose from the two forms of the verb in brackets to write out the following sentences correctly.
   (a) Most car drivers (like, likes) to travel in fine weather.
   (b) The passengers (was, were) in the back seats.
   (c) The driver (was, were) wearing a seat belt.
   (d) The taxis at the station (look, looks) fine in their new colours.
   (e) The taxi drivers (has, have) a charity football match to play today.

Another rule to remember is that the words *each*, *every*, *either* and *neither*, when they refer to two persons or things, must always be followed by the singular form of the verb.

e.g. *Each* of the taxi drivers *has* a licence for his taxi.
Every one of the taxi-drivers does *his* best to provide a good service.
Either Fiona or Nikki *has* your book.
Neither Naila nor Tabasin *knows* anything about it.

17 Choose from the two forms of the verb in brackets to write out the following sentences correctly.
   (a) Every member of the class (has, have) been asked to attend.
   (b) Neither of the girls offered (her, their) help at lunchtime.
   (c) Each of the runners (was, were) within the time for the four-minute mile.
   (d) Either of the two boys (is, are) to blame for what happened.

There are three other rules that need to be learnt about the singular and plural forms of a verb. The first two rules are:

- When two singular nouns are joined by *with* or *as well as* the verb is always singular.
  e.g. Kamela, *as well as* Urmila, *is* late for school.
  Melanie, *with* Angela, *is* on holiday.
- When two singular nouns are joined by *and* the verb is plural.
  e.g. The captain *and* his crew *were* rescued.
  At night Sarah *and* her sister *do* their homework.

18 Now choose the correct form of verb from those in brackets and write out the following sentences.
   (a) Mary, with her dog, (walk, walks) in the park.
   (b) The pilot and his passengers (were, was) rescued after the plane force-landed in the Sahara.
   (c) Every morning Michelle, with her sister, (catch, catches) the bus to school.
   (d) The Headmistress and her staff (were, was) organising a disco for the fourth year.

The third and last rule in this group is for the collective noun.
These are nouns used to name a collection of persons or things considered as a whole.

e.g. an *army* of soldiers
a *colony* of gulls
a *horde* of savages
a *plague* of locusts
a *shoal* of herrings
a *troupe* of dancers

The problem with collective nouns is that they can be either singular or plural according to the sense in which the writer uses them. For example, an audience is sometimes thought of as a single body and the noun is then followed by a singular verb.

e.g. The audience *was* composed entirely of women.

At other times an audience is looked upon as a number of separate people, and in that case it is followed by a plural verb.

e.g. The audience *were* urged to keep *their* seats.

19 Write out the following sentences and insert the correct form of the verb according to the sense in which the collective noun is used.
(a) The SAS (consist, consists) of men specially picked and trained.
(b) The committee (has, have) decided to appoint a new secretary.
(c) The public (is, are) requested to keep the park free from litter.
(d) The crew of the sinking yacht (was, were) picked up by a rescue helicopter.
(e) A crowd of holidaymakers (was, were) walking towards the beach.

20 Write out the following sentences and fill in the missing verbs.
(a) It . . . a wonderful sight and both girls . . . delighted.
(b) Both Darren and Jason . . . absent from school.
(c) The captain and his crew . . . saved but the ship . . . lost.
(d) Neither of the boys . . . fit enough for games.
(e) Everyone . . . delighted with the performance.
(f) Nobody . . . more pleased than I.
(g) The Papuan tribe, which . . . once a source of trouble, . . . now loyal to the government.
(h) A line of tall, slim poplars . . . the approach to the house.
(i) The leader, together with a number of his followers, . . . placed under arrest.
(j) The prince and princess, along with a party of guests, . . . returning to London.

Talking and listening

21 Form groups of four or five.
Think about the following five words written by Carl Sandburg the American poet:

A word has long shadows

Discuss the idea that some words we read and hear, stay in our minds and make us happy, sad or angry. Ask each member of the group to tell of words that make him or her feel strongly — words that have emotional meanings.
Make a group list of such words under the headings happy, sad and angry.
Choose a member of the group to tell the remainder of the class about the list.
Class discussion: Are there 'dangerous' words that can influence us?

Learning at home

22 Mrs Malaprop, one of the characters in Sheridan's play, *The Rivals*, was very fond of using long words. Unfortunately, she often used the wrong one. Here she is talking about her daughter's education:

As she grew up I should have her instructed in geometry, that she might know something of the contagious countries.

Can you correct this?
Mrs Malaprop has given her name to mistakes like this, for we call them *malapropisms*.
Correct the following modern malapropisms.
(a) How dare you talk to me like that! Just what are you incinerating?
(b) When we get to Greece we shall have to change our money into draculas.
(c) The patient in Ward Four has had a sirloin drip attached to his arm.
(d) Prices in the shops today are absolutely exuberant.
(e) To make these sweets we shall need a packet of desecrated coconut and a can of exasperated milk.

23 Dr Spooner was an Oxford don who got his words mixed up in a special kind of way.
When he was talking he would often change the order of the first letters of words or even whole words.
For example, it is said that he once asked a waitress for '*a bath of milk and a glass bun*'.
Write down what you think the speaker meant to say in each of the following *spoonerisms*.

(a) It's five miles as the flow cries.
(b) Darren has a well boiled icicle.
(c) Please let me sew you to a sheet.
(d) The baby is always knighting her bails.
(e) Cheap tray dips to the coast.
(f) Mr Aubrey bakes the toys for woodwork.
(g) It is roaring with pain today. That fine feather warcast was wrong.

Book Review

THE TURBULENT TERM OF TYKE TILER by Gene Kemp

Plot

Bright and boisterous Tyke Tiler (12) and dim but endearing Danny Price are in their last term at Cricklepit School. The story is a series of their adventures. Danny is always getting into trouble, but is too slow-thinking to help himself. Tyke tries to put matters right, but often ends up with the blame.

Danny's scrapes include taking a £10 note and letting his pet mouse loose in assembly. Tyke's adventures include stealing an examination paper to make sure Danny will do well enough to prevent his removal to a special school, and also secret fights with Kneeshaw.

Things are going well towards the end of term. Stunning Miss Honeywell, the student teacher, gets the class doing a play about King Arthur, and has chosen Danny for Sir Galahad. He is thrilled by this and resolves to stop stealing. However, Tyke falls ill, and Kneeshaw bullies the now unprotected Danny. Tyke returns to school to find Danny has run off, accused of stealing a gold watch found in his bag. Tyke finds Danny at their hideout in the old mill. Danny insists that Kneeshaw has 'framed' him. Tyke goes to the Head to make a bargain: Danny's whereabouts revealed, in return for Kneeshaw's confession. The Head is taken aback but eventually agrees and Kneeshaw admits the blame.

In the last day of term, Tyke suddenly decides to climb up the outside of the bell tower. An audience gathers, and just as Tyke is about to descend, the most unpopular of the teachers yells out that Theodora Tiler should come down at once. Tyke, who loathes her real name, rings the bell in defiance, only to find the roof collapse beneath her. Teacher Will Merchant 'writes' the end of the story, telling how Tyke recovered from her injuries and told him all about her turbulent term.

Background

Mr Tiler is an engine driver, Mrs Tiler a nurse. Brother Spud is fourteen and sister Beryl is eighteen. The family atmosphere is warm, noisy and argumentative; they are not well-off, but are comfortable, happy and active. Mr Tiler stands for the council but we are spared any political issues. Danny's home is not so happy: his mother has little time for him, and his father is in jail. Both children are happy at school, and most of their teachers are understanding and caring.

Language

The story is told by Tyke and this helps to conceal her sex until the last chapter. The language level of the book is thus well within the 11-year-old range. There is plenty of dialogue, and the style is often like neat, sharp, amusing conversation.

Interests

Love: The friendship between Tyke and Danny is a firm partnership. Tyke is devoted to Danny, and takes all sorts of risks for him. She is also infuriated by him, and when he is too much of a nuisance, she thumps him quiet. Beryl's romance with Richard is mentioned now and then, usually for Tyke to make fun of it.
Humour is plentiful, and to set the tone each chapter starts with a short classroom joke. A lot of the humour comes from a lively telling of the story and Tyke's irritation with Danny.
Violence arises only in the form of fights with Kneeshaw. However, Tyke takes a beating now and then, as when she falls in the river, or when she tumbles from the school roof.

Characterisation

Tyke and Danny are an attractive and believable pair, with some real concern for each other. Other main characters are dealt with briefly but stay in the mind. An example is Mr Merchant's performance in his classroom.

Themes include undergoing risks and taking blame for friendship's sake, and the book shows how contact between the bright and not so bright can help both. Also of interest is the fact that Tyke is not revealed as a girl until the very end: many readers will have thought she was a boy.

This Carnegie Medal winner is easy to obtain and is a sensitive, warm-hearted and amusing book. A lovely read for everybody.
Puffin, 1979 116 pages ISBN 0 14 03.1135 1

adapted from *Bookpage*

Questions to answer

1 (a) Write out the meaning of each of the following words, then
(b) use each word in a sentence of your own.

turbulent endearing dialogue
boisterous issues sensitive

2 Tyke often ends up with the blame. Why is this so?
3 What made Tyke steal an examination paper?
4 What makes Danny decide to stop stealing?
5 How was Danny 'framed'?
6 What made Tyke ring the bell?
7 Tell in your own words what the Tiler family was like.
8 How does Tyke show her devotion to Danny?
9 What makes the book easy to read?
10 What makes it a humorous book?
11 Why would readers think that Tyke was a boy?
12 Which important prize has this book won?

Writing

13 (a) Make a list of not more than TEN books of any kind you have read in the last year. Include those you have read in school and at home.
(b) Pick ONE of the books you have listed and write what you enjoyed about it and why you would recommend it to a friend.

14 Write about your favourite television star. Mention the programme, the channel and the time he or she can be seen.
You might point out his/her age, looks and dress: your reasons for choosing him/her as your favourite: other shows he/she is in and any other interesting facts you know about him/her.

15 Your mother sees you reading your favourite magazine and asks if you haven't anything better to do. Write the argument you would give for reading your magazine.

16 What book have you seen serialised on television? Say what you thought of the book on screen. Had you read the book before or did you go on to read it? How did the television version affect you?

17 Name four magazines you take or would like to take every week. What makes them your favourites?

18 If you were being given a book as a present or a prize, what would you choose and why?

Talking and listening

19 Form groups of five.
Spend some time working on both of the following.

(a) *Top paperbacks*
Discuss, agree and then make a group list of ten top paperbacks.
For each title write a quotation that would attract readers, e.g.

'A good fast read of gun-running, smuggling and murder.'

Transfer list and quotations to a larger sheet of paper for display on the classroom wall.

(b) *Selling a book*
Design (1) a cover, and (2) an advertising poster for a paperback called *Wild Fire*.
Cut out and paste items and lettering from colour magazines if the group is not artistic.
Remember that the idea is to sell the book to other people.
The poster opposite may suggest ideas.

20 Form groups of five.
Discuss the writing of an historical romance.
Decide upon:

the period of history
the main characters
the setting
any exciting events

As a group exercise write a short account of the plot and the first chapter.

Language—synonyms, antonyms and homonyms

A *Synonyms* are words having nearly the same meaning and use.

Our language is rich in synonyms because it comes from many other languages, e.g. Greek, Latin and French, and a word with the same meaning has been borrowed from each. For example:

holiday (Old English) and *vacation* (Latin)
child (Old English) and *infant* (Norman French)

Not many synonyms have exactly the same meaning and use. For example, being *manly* is not quite the same as being *virile*. It is therefore important to pick the right synonym for the sentence you are writing.

21 Here is a list of synonyms meaning more or less the same thing.

mob congregation crowd audience spectators assembly

Knockouts
Exciting reading for young people
DAVID REES
WAVES
Alan C McLean
It's only rock 'n' roll
WILL OF IRON
Gerard Melia
WALKING SHADOWS
TERRY DEARY
A TASTE OF FREEDOM
JULIUS LESTER
A Taste of Freedom
We are pleased to introduce readers in the UK to A Taste of Freedom which Julius Lester has written specially for Knockouts.
Three stories of courage and endurance set in the American south before the emancipation of slaves.
"based on the lives of the unknown people who are the ones who truly make history. I love trying to recreate history in an imaginative way. Since I was a child I have been obsessed with trying to put myself inside people who lived before I was born"
Julius Lester
Longman

Use a dictionary to find and write down the meaning of each of the seven words.

22 Find two synonyms for each of the following words.

tired stop change keep terror meal

23 Rearrange the following words in PAIRS of synonyms.

forgive leader haughty haste
slap chief fool wanderer end
proud forfeit finish pardon
rover rogue smack dolt hurry
fine rascal

B *Antonyms* are words of opposite meaning. Thus *pain* is the antonym of *pleasure*.
The antonym of a word can often be made by adding to it a prefix, e.g.

dis	appear	disappear
un	certain	uncertain
in	audible	inaudible

but antonyms, like synonyms, may be completely different words. Also like synonyms, there may be several of them, and each with a slightly different meaning, e.g.

clever — dull, stupid, backward, slow

24 Find two antonyms for each of the following.

retreat expand unite increase
entrance guilty

25 For each of the words in (a) find an antonym in (b).

(a)	superior	transparent
	wither	wax
	strange	hinder
	permanent	freedom
	vague	absence
(b)	presence	bondage
	familiar	temporary
	grow	opaque
	wane	inferior
	help	definite

26 Give each of the following words an opposite meaning by adding a prefix.

modest logical defensible
gratitude agree regular
soluble finite possible
understand fiction centralise

C *Homonyms* are words having the same spelling but different meanings. Thus, *bark* means the covering of a tree trunk and the cry of a dog.
Here are some more examples of homonyms:

bear	=	animal; to carry
fair	=	market; beautiful; reasonable
bank	=	place where money is kept; sloping ground
host	=	a large number of people; landlord of an inn; entertainer of guests

27 Copy out the following homonyms and for each one give two different meanings. You may need to look the words up in a dictionary.

charger stole tick pole fry
hop leaves port till corn
sheer submit prone assume

D *Homophones* are words of the same sound but of different spelling and meaning, e.g. *rain*, *reign* and *rein* or *piece* and *peace*.
Here are some more examples:

right	=	correct
rite	=	solemn ceremony
write	=	to set down on paper
meet	=	to encounter
meat	=	flesh used as food
mete	=	to portion out or allot
bald	=	hairless
bawled	=	shouted

28 Use the following homophones in sentences to bring out clearly their difference in meaning.

wane	wain	sweet	suite
vane	vein	wrote	rote
there	their	knead	need

Finally, you need not remember to distinguish between *homonyms* and *homophones*. Today the word *homonym* is nearly always used for both.

Poetry

Comic and curious

Tales

Word power

Jabberwocky

'Twas brillig, and the slithy toves
Did gyre and gimble in the wabe;
All mimsy were the borogoves,
And the mome raths outgrabe.

'Beware the Jabberwock, my son!
The jaws that bite, the claws that catch!
Beware the Jubjub bird, and shun
The *frumious* Bandersnatch!'

He took his *vorpal* sword in hand:
Long time the *manxome* foe he sought—
So rested he by the Tumtum tree,
And stood awhile in thought.

And as in *uffish* thought he stood,
The Jabberwock, with eyes of flame,
Came *whiffling* through the *tulgey* wood,
And burbled as it came!

One, two! One, two! And through and through
The vorpal blade went snicker-snack!
He left it dead, and with its head
He went *galumphing* back.

Activities

1 Read the extract from *Alice in Wonderland* on pages 64–5. Imagine you are Humpty Dumpty. Explain to Alice the portmanteau words in the poem which are in *italics*.

2 Tell in your own words the story of *Jabberwocky*.

Here are some more verses by Lewis Carroll. They were read as evidence at the trial of the Knave of Hearts. In Alice's opinion there was not an atom of meaning in them.

They Told Me You Had Been to Her

They told me you had been to her,
  And mentioned me to him:
She gave me a good character,
  But said I could not swim.

He sent them word I had not gone
  (We know it to be true):
If she should push the matter on
  What would become of you?

I gave her one, they gave him two,
  You gave us three or more;
They all returned from him to you,
  Though they were mine before.

If I or she should chance to be
  Involved in this affair,
He trusts to you to set them free,
  Exactly as we were.

My notion was that you had been
  (Before she had this fit)
An obstacle that came between
  Him, and ourselves, and it.

Don't let him know she liked them best,
  For this must ever be
A secret, kept from all the rest,
  Between yourself and me.

Activity

1 Do you agree or disagree with Alice? Give two or three reasons.

'Sir, what is poetry?'
'Why, Sir, it is much easier to say what it is not. We all *know* what light is, but it is not easy to *tell* what it is.'

Samuel Johnson

The best definition of poetry was probably given by Samuel Taylor Coleridge. He said that poetry was 'the best words in the best order'.

Remember this definition when you look at a poem. Always check that the words are the best for the job they have to do.

In this poem W H Davies has chosen the kind of words we use every day to put across a simple rule for living in a world that is rushed and noisy.

Leisure

What is this life if, full of care,
We have no time to stand and stare?

No time to stand beneath the boughs
And stare as long as sheep or cows.

No time to see, in broad daylight,
Streams full of stars, like skies at night.

No time to turn at Beauty's glance,
And watch her feet, how they can dance.

No time to wait till her mouth can
Enrich that smile her eyes began.

A poor life this if, full of care,
We have no time to stand and stare.

W H Davies

Cargoes

Quinquireme of Nineveh from distant Ophir
Rowing home to haven in sunny Palestine,
With a cargo of ivory,
And apes and peacocks,
Sandalwood, cedarwood, and sweet white wine.

Stately Spanish galleon coming from the Isthmus,
Dipping through the Tropics by the palm-green shores,
With a cargo of diamonds,
Emeralds, amethysts,
Topazes, and cinnamon, and gold moidores.

Dirty British coaster with a salt-caked smoke stack
Butting through the Channel in the mad March days,
With a cargo of Tyne coal,
Road-rail, pig-lead,
Firewood, iron-ware, and cheap tin trays.

John Masefield

Activities

1 Would this have been a better poem if the words had been more 'poetic' and 'flowery'? Give your reasons.
2 Would the poem have been as good if Davies had used portmanteau words? Can you say why?

Cargoes is another poem with well-chosen words.
It is about ships and their cargoes. The word *ships* is not in the poem because Masefield felt it was not quite right. Instead, he gives three clear pictures of *types* of ships:

quinquireme of Nineveh
stately Spanish *galleon*
dirty British *coaster*

The cargoes are described with equal care. All the romance and glamour of the East is in:

. . . a cargo of ivory,
And apes and peacocks,
Sandalwood, cedarwood, and sweet white wine.

Then the colour and splendid wealth of the Spanish Main follows:

. . . a cargo of diamonds,
Emeralds, amethysts,
Topazes, and cinnamon, and gold moidores.

In contrast, there is the grimy but necessary cargo carried around our shores every day:

. . . Tyne coal,
Road-rail, pig-lead,
Firewood, iron-ware, and cheap tin trays.

Activities

Remember to ask these questions whenever you have to write or talk about the words, or *diction*, of a poem.

- Have the right words been chosen by the poet?
- Does every word count or are there too many?
- Are the words simple and natural or are they too 'poetic'?
- Do any of the words stay in your mind? Are they vivid and memorable?
- Do you hear any kind of 'music' or rhythm in the words when they are spoken aloud?

One of the best-known poems in the English language is *The Daffodils* by William Wordsworth.

Read it and then answer these questions.

- What is the poem about?
- What kind of experience is Wordsworth writing about?
- What is the meaning of the poem?

An answer to any of these questions will give you what is known as the *theme* of the poem.

The Daffodils

I wandered lonely as a cloud
That floats on high o'er vales and hills,
When all at once I saw a crowd,
A host, of golden daffodils;
Beside the lake, beneath the trees,
Fluttering and dancing in the breeze.

Continuous as the stars that shine
And twinkle on the milky way,
They stretched in never-ending line
Along the margin of a bay:
Ten thousand saw I at a glance,
Tossing their heads in sprightly dance.

The waves beside them danced; but they
Out-did the sparkling waves in glee:
A poet could not but be gay,
In such a jocund company:
I gazed—and gazed—but little thought
What wealth the show to me had brought:

For oft, when on my couch I lie
In vacant or in pensive mood,
They flash upon that inward eye
Which is the bliss of solitude;
And then my heart with pleasure fills,
And dances with the daffodils.

William Wordsworth

Activities

1 Tell in your own words the *theme* of each of the following poems.
   (a) *The Daffodils*
   (b) *Leisure*
   (c) *Cargoes*

2 Wordsworth claims in the poem that he 'wandered lonely as a cloud' when in fact his sister Dorothy was with him on that walk in 1802. She wrote about it in her Journal entry (see pages 87–8) for Thursday, April 15th.
   (a) Look at the poem and the entry and say how they are the same and how they are different. For example, Dorothy's account ends with resting, but William's with dancing.
   (b) Which do you think is better, the prose or the poetry? Give reasons for your choice.

Weird and wicked

The Hairy Toe

Once there was a woman went out to pick beans,
and she found a Hairy Toe.
She took the Hairy Toe home with her,
and that night, when she went to bed,
the wind began to moan and groan.
Away off in the distance
she seemed to hear a voice crying,
'Where's my Hair-r-ry To-o-oe?
Who's got my Hair-r-ry To-o-oe?'
The woman scrooched down,
'way down under the covers,
and about that time
the wind appeared to hit the house,
smoosh,

and the old house creaked and cracked
like something was trying to get in.
The voice had come nearer,
almost at the door now,
and it said,
'Where's my Hair-r-ry To-o-oe?
Who's got my Hair-r-ry To-o-oe?'
The woman scrooched further down
under the covers
and pulled them tight around her head.

The wind growled around the house
like some big animal
and r-r-umbled
over the chimney.
All at once she heard the door cr-r-a-ack
And Something slipped in
and began to creep over the floor.
The floor went
cre-e-eak, cre-e-eak
at every step that thing took towards her bed.
The woman could almost feel
it bending over her head.
There in an awful voice it said:
'Where's my Hair-r-ry To-o-oe?
Who's got my Hair-r-ry To-o-oe?

You've got it!'

traditional American

The Two Ravens

As I was walking all alone,
I heard two ravens cry and moan:
I heard the one to the other say,
'Where shall we go and dine today?'

'In the ditch below the field
There lies a knight that's newly killed;
And nobody knows that he lies there
But his hawk, his hound, and his lady fair.

'His hound has gone to hunt the deer,
His hawk has flown to the empty air,
His lady's found another man;
So we'll have dinner while we can.

'His white neck-bone will be your prize,
And I'll pick out his two blue eyes;
With one lock of his golden hair
We'll line our nest, when it is bare.

'Many a man for him will mourn,
But none shall know where he has gone;
Over his bones, when they are bare,
The wind shall blow for evermore.'

Ian Serraillier
from the Old Scottish Ballad *The Twa Corbies*

Shadwell Stair

I am the ghost of Shadwell Stair.
Along the wharves by the water-house,
And through the dripping slaughter-house,
I am the shadow that walks there.

Yet I have flesh both firm and cool,
And eyes tumultuous as the gems
Of moons and lamps in the lapping Thames
When dusk sails wavering down the pool.

Shuddering the purple street-arc burns
Where I watch always; from the banks
Dolorously the shipping clanks,
And after me a strange tide turns.

I walk till the stars of London wane
And dawn creeps up the Shadwell Stair.
But when the crowing sirens blare
I with another ghost am lain.

Wilfred Owen

The Knifesmith

I am the man who made the knife
That killed the king of Babylon;
It had a sheath of beaten gold,
And in its haft strange jewels shone.

I wrought it through the winter days,
And when they brightened into spring
I led it to the light, and knew
It was a dagger for a king.

I sent it humbly to the king,
As being fit for him to wear;
His page-boy brought it back to me:
"The king has daggers and to spare."

But while I dozed beside my fire,
Beside my fire, as night drew on,
A hand came rustling through the wall
And seized the dagger and was gone.

Next morning when the king was dead,
  And princes snarling in his hall,
The dagger he had scorned to wear
  Was back upon my workshop wall.

And seeing it upon my wall,
  And knowing that the king was dead,
How could I turn to making knives
  For chopping meat or cutting bread?

No, I shall wear it at my side,
  And wander through the world, until
On some auspicious night, we find
  Another king for it to kill.

Dorothy Howard

Rhythm

There is a regular beat to poetry, just as there is a regular beat to our hearts.
This beat is called *rhythm*.
Read aloud several times the lines that follow.

I sprang to the stirrup, and Jorris, and he:
I galloped, Dirck galloped, we galloped all three;
'God speed!' cried the watch, as the gate bolts undrew;
'Speed!' echoed the wall to us galloping through;

The rhythm here is of a hoof-beat to suggest the galloping of horses. It was used by Robert Browning in a poem about three horsemen setting out to bring important news to another town.

1 Read aloud one or two verses from *Hunter Trials* (page 127). What does the rhythm of these verses suggest to you?
2 Read *Night Mail* (page 135) and notice how the poet alters the speed of the rhythm to suit the changing speed of the train as it crosses the Border into Scotland.
Write a short piece about the rhythms in this poem.

Here and there

A Summer Farm

Straws like tame lightnings lie about the grass
And hang zig-zag on hedges. Green as glass
The water in the horse-trough shines.
Nine ducks go wobbling by in two straight lines.

A hen stares at nothing with one eye,
Then picks it up. Out of an empty sky
A swallow falls and, flickering through
The barn, dives up again into the dizzy blue.

I lie, not thinking, in the cool soft grass,
Afraid of where a thought might take me—as
The grasshopper with plated face
Unfolds his legs and finds himself in space.

Norman MacCaig

Activities

'Straws like tame lightning lie about the grass . . .'

These eight words are used to paint a picture in the mind of the reader.
The poet joins two very different things with the word *like* in order to compare them.
Such a comparison is called a *simile.*
Here are other examples.

> The country road writhed *like* a snake.
> The women at the bargain counter fought *like* wild cats.
> The scar was *like* a red crack across ice.

'. . . Green as glass
The water in the horse-trough shines.'

Here is another simile, but this time the joining word is *as.*

In a simile either *like* or *as* may be used as joining words. Here are similes that use *as.*

> A mind as sharp *as* a needle
> A dancer light *as* thistledown
> Hair as smooth *as* silk

1 Look again at the two similes from the poem. How good are these word pictures? Are they strong and vivid enough to stay in your mind?

> Do bent or twisted straws lying on grass look like forked lightning that has lost its energy and power?
>
> Does water in a horse-trough shine like some kinds of green glass?

2 Copy out these two similes and below each one say what you think of it as a word picture.

Preludes (I)

The winter evening settles down
With smells of steaks in passageways.
Six o'clock.
The burnt-out ends of smoky days.
And now a gusty shower wraps
The grimy scraps
Of withered leaves about your feet
And newspapers from vacant lots;
The showers beat
On broken blinds and chimney-pots,
And at the corner of the street
A lonely cab-horse steams and stamps.
And then the lighting of the lamps.

T S Eliot

Activities

1 'The burnt-out ends of smoky days.'

Here is another picture in words.
The poet is comparing the early evening of a winter's day to a cigarette-end (or possibly a candle-end).
Note that the early evening is not *like* a cigarette-end but actually *is* one.
The comparison does not use the words *like* or *as* so it cannot be a simile. What it does is to liken one thing to another by saying it is that thing.
Such expressions are called *metaphors*.
Here are more examples.

I will speak daggers to her.
(I will stab her with words.)
The camel is the ship of the desert.
The car sailed along the road.

Copy out the metaphor from the poem and then say what you think of it as a word picture.

2 Copy out the metaphors below and for each one say what you think of it and why.

The leaden clouds hang heavily.
A mountain of a man came storming into the bar.

3 Imagine you are to take five black and white photographs of the scene in the poem. Take words or lines from the poem as titles for each of the photographs, e.g.

Photograph 5 A lonely cab-horse steams and stamps. (line 12)

Winter the Huntsman

Through his iron glades
Rides Winter the Huntsman.
All colour fades
As his horn is heard sighing.

Far through the forest
His wild hooves crash and thunder
Till many a mighty branch
Is torn asunder.

And the red reynard creeps
To his hole near the river,
The copper leaves fall
And the bare trees shiver,

As night creeps from the ground,
Hides each tree from its brother,
And each dying sound
Reveals yet another.

Is it Winter the Huntsman
Who gallops through his iron glades,
Cracking his cruel whip
To the gathering shades?

Osbert Sitwell

Activities

1 'Through his iron glades
Rides Winter the Huntsman.'

This is a metaphor with a difference. Here, and throughout the poem, Winter is said to be not a season but a person. This giving of human qualities to anything that is not human is called *personification*. Other examples are:

The oaks forgot their whispering.
The yellow smoke rubbed its nose against the window pane.
Green-eyed jealousy has walked among us.

Copy out these examples of personification and for each one say what you think of it as a word picture.

2 We have now looked at the three most common types of word picture: simile, metaphor and personification.
They are used in poetry to make a picture or image flash into our minds. For this reason another term for word pictures is *imagery*.
Look through other poems in this part of the book to find and write out examples of the three types of imagery. Identify each one and say what you think of it.

3 When you write about a poem it is helpful to remember the word TIDE.
The letters in this word will remind you of:

Theme
Imagery
Diction
Enjoyment

Learn to answer the questions under each of these headings and you will be able to write something about any poem.

Theme
What was the poem about?
Was the meaning clear?

Imagery
What word pictures did the poet use?
Are those pictures vivid, strong and clear?
Does the imagery help the reader understand the poet's feelings?

Diction
Have the right words been chosen?
Does every word count or are there too many?

Are any of the words vivid and memorable?

Enjoyment
Did the poem make you:
feel happy or sad?
think more deeply about a problem?
understand yourself or other people better?

The word TIDE may remind you of the rhythm of the sea and that a poem also has rhythm.

Use the word TIDE to help you write about any poem of your choice. Aim for four paragraphs: one for each of the headings above.

Here is a poem to be spoken aloud and with a part for everyone.
Parts should be organised as follows.

- Divide class into two equal groups containing both girls and boys. These groups are GROUP 1 and GROUP 2 in the poem.
- Choose the solo parts: DANIEL, DARIUS, MOTHER, SWEETHEART, VOICE OF GOD from GROUP 1.
- Choose the solo parts: A, B, C, D, E, F from GROUP 2.
- All boys in the class to take the part of the LIONS. (Some practice in growling may be needed!)

Now your teacher will read the poem aloud. Check the lines you will speak whilst this is being done.

Finally, rehearse the poem with the help and advice of your teacher.

When you are expert and well-skilled at speaking the poem you might think of a public performance.

Daniel

A Negro's interpretation of the Bible story

GROUP 1 Darius the Mede was a king and a wonder.
His eye was proud, and his voice was thunder.
He kept bad lions in a monstrous den.
He fed up the lions on Christian men.

GROUP 2 Daniel was the chief hired man of the land.

A He stirred up the music in the palace band.
B He whitewashed the cellar.
C He shovelled in the coal.

GROUP 2 And Daniel kept a-praying:

DANIEL Lord save my soul!

GROUP 2 Daniel kept a-praying:

DANIEL Lord save my soul!

GROUP 2 Daniel kept a-praying:

DANIEL Lord save my soul!

GROUP 2 Daniel was a butler, swagger and swell.

A He ran up the stairs.
B He answered the bell.
C And *he* would let in whoever came a-calling—
Saints so holy, scamps so appalling.

A Old man Ahab leaves his card.
B Elisha and the bears are a-waiting in the yard.
C Here comes Pharaoh and his snakes a-calling.
D Here comes Cain and his wife a-calling.
E Shadrach, Meshach and Abednego for tea.
F Here comes Jonah, and the Whale—

GROUP 1 And the SEA!

GROUP 2 And Daniel kept a-praying:

DANIEL Lord save my soul!

GROUP 1 Daniel kept a-praying:

DANIEL Lord save my soul!

GROUP 2 Daniel kept a-praying:

DANIEL Lord save my soul!

GROUP 1 His sweetheart and his mother were Christian and meek.
They washed and ironed for Darius every week.
One Thursday he met them at the door:
Paid them as usual, but acted sore.
He said:

DARIUS Your Daniel is a dead little pigeon.
He's a good hard worker, but he talks religion.

GROUP 2 And he showed them Daniel in the lions' cage,
Daniel standing quietly, the lions in a rage.

A His good old mother cried:

MOTHER Lord save him!

B And Daniel's tender sweetheart cried:

SWEETHEART Lord save him!

GROUP 1 And she was a golden lily in the dew.
And she was as sweet as an apple on the tree,
And she was as fine as a melon in the cornfield,
Gliding and lovely as a ship on the sea,
Gliding and lovely as a ship on the sea.
And she prayed to the Lord:

SWEETHEART Send Gabriel. Send Gabriel.

GROUP 2 King Darius said to the lions:

DARIUS Bite Daniel. Bite Daniel.
Bite him. Bite him. Bite him!

GROUP 1 Thus roared the lions:

LIONS We want Daniel, Daniel, Daniel,
We want Daniel, Daniel, Daniel.
Grrr—rrr—rrr . . .

A And Daniel did not frown,
Daniel did not cry.

B He kept on looking at the sky.

GROUP 2 And the Lord said unto Gabriel:

VOICE OF GOD Go chain the lions down,
Go chain the lions down,
Go chain the lions down,
Go chain the lions down.

GROUP 1 And Gabriel chained the lions,
And Gabriel chained the lions,
And Gabriel chained the lions.

GROUP 2 And Daniel got out of the den,
And Daniel got out of the den,
And Daniel got out of the den.

GROUP 1 And Darius said:

DARIUS You're a Christian child.

GROUP 1 Darius said:

DARIUS You're a Christian child.

GROUP 1 Darius said:

DARIUS You're a Christian child.

GROUP 2 And gave him his job again,

GROUP 1 And gave him his job again,

EVERYONE And gave him his job again.

Vachel Lindsay

Rhyme

'Darius the Mede was a king and a *wonder*.
His eye was proud, and his voice was *thunder*.'

When lines end in similar sounds like this we call it *rhyme*.

Poems that use rhyme do so to a plan or a *scheme*:

'Darius the Mede was a king and a *wonder*.	A
His eye was proud, and his voice was *thunder*.	A
He kept bad lions in a monstrous *den*.	B
He fed up the lions on Christian *men*.'	B

A different plan, that of A B B A, is used for *Hunter Trials* on page 127.

1 Look up the following poems and write out the rhyming scheme for each one:

Shadwell Stair (page 117)
A Snake Yarn (page 134)
The Daffodils (page 114) (another letter of the alphabet will be needed for this scheme)

2 Form groups of six to collect greetings cards (Christmas, Birthday, etc.). Check the verses in your collection to find out:

if rhyming is very popular,
the rhyming scheme most used,
whether most verses are good or bad.

Write a group report on your findings.

My Mother Saw a Dancing Bear

My mother saw a dancing bear
By the schoolyard, a day in June.
The keeper stood with chain and bar
And whistle-pipe, and played a tune.

And bruin lifted up its head
And lifted up its dusty feet,
And all the children laughed to see
It caper in the summer heat.

They watched as for the Queen it died.
They watched it march. They watched it halt.
They heard the keeper as he cried,
'Now, roly-poly!' 'Somersault!'

And then, my mother said, there came
The keeper with a begging-cup,
The bear with burning coat of fur,
Shaming the laughter to a stop.

They paid a penny for the dance,
But what they saw was not the show;
Only, in bruin's aching eyes,
Far distant forests, and the snow.

Charles Causley

Comic and curious

The Fight of the Year

'And there goes the bell for the third month
and Winter comes out of its corner looking groggy
Spring leads with a left to the head
followed by a sharp right to the body
    daffodils
    primroses
    crocuses
    snowdrops
    lilacs
    violets
    pussywillow
Winter can't take much more punishment
and Spring shows no signs of tiring
    tadpoles
    squirrels
    baalambs
    badgers
    bunny rabbits
    mad march hares
    horses and hounds
Spring is merciless

Winter won't go the full twelve rounds
    bobtail clouds
    scallywaggy winds
    the sun
    a pavement artist
    in every town
A left to the chin
and Winter's down!
      1 tomatoes
      2 radish
      3 cucumber
      4 onions
      5 beetroot
      6 celery
      7 and any
      8 amount
      9 of lettuce
      10 for dinner
Winter's out for the count
Spring is the winner!'

Roger McGough

. . . . LABORIOUS WORK . . . .

. . . . . AND CAREFUL GROOMING . . . .

. . . . ARE AMPLY REPAID . . . . .

. . . . . BY THE THRILL OF ATTENDING . . . . . .

. . . . A GYMKHANA

Hunter Trials

It's awf'lly bad luck on Diana,
  Her ponies have swallowed their bits;
She fished down their throats with a spanner
  And frightened them all into fits.

So now she's attempting to borrow.
  Do lend her some bits, Mummy, *do*;
I'll lend her my own for to-morrow,
  But to-day *I*'ll be wanting them too.

Just look at Prunella on Guzzle,
  The wizardest pony on earth;
Why doesn't she slacken his muzzle?
  And tighten the breech in his girth?

I say, Mummy, there's Mrs Geyser
  And doesn't she look pretty sick?
I bet it's because Mona Lisa
  Was hit on the hock with a brick.

Miss Blewitt says Monica threw it,
  But Monica says it was Joan,
And Joan's very thick with Miss Blewitt,
  So Monica's sulking alone.

And Margaret failed in her paces,
  Her withers got tied in a noose,
So her coronets caught in the traces
  And now all her fetlocks are loose.

Oh, it's me now. I'm terribly nervous.
  I wonder if Smudges will shy.
She's practically certain to swerve as
  Her Pelham is over one eye.

Oh wasn't it naughty of Smudges?
  Oh, Mummy, I'm sick with disgust.
She threw me in front of the Judges,
  And my silly old collarbone's bust.

John Betjeman

Mr Kartoffel

Mr Kartoffel's a whimsical man;
He drinks his beer from a watering-can,
And for no good reason that I can see
He fills his pockets with china tea.
He parts his hair with a knife and fork
And takes his ducks for a Sunday walk.
Says he, 'If my wife and I should choose
To wear our stockings outside our shoes,
Plant tulip-bulbs in the baby's pram
And eat tobacco instead of jam,
And fill the bath with cauliflowers,
That's nobody's business at all but ours.'

Says Mrs K, 'I may choose to travel
With a sack of grass or a sack of gravel,
Or paint my toes, one black one white,
Or sit on a bird's nest half the night—
But whatever I do that is rum or rare,
I rather think that it's my affair.
So fill up your pockets with stamps and string,
And let us be ready for anything!'
Says Mr K to his whimsical wife,
'How can we face the storms of life,
Unless we are ready for anything?'

James Reeves

A Small Dragon

I've found a small dragon in the woodshed.
Think it must have come from deep inside a forest
because it's damp and green and leaves
are still reflecting in its eyes.

I fed it on many things, tried grass,
the roots of stars, hazel-nut and dandelion,
but it stared up at me as if to say, I need
foods you can't provide.

It made a nest among the coal,
not unlike a bird's but larger,
it is out of place here
and is quite silent.

If you believe in it I would come
hurrying to your house to let you share my wonder,
but I want instead to see
if you yourself will pass this way.

Brian Patten

Activity
Why not make a poetry poster? Copy out this poem on to a large sheet of plain paper and then illustrate or decorate it.

Falcon's End

He was old.
He was in the Winter of his time.
Old and tired.
His great brown and white wings
Were not as strong as they had once been.
And the deep-set eyes in his black capped head
Were not as sharp as before.

The old falcon had been flying a long while,
Heading south, away from the cold.
He had made the flight many times before.
But this year he had lost his way.
Now he was tired.
Old and tired.
He needed rest. He needed food.

Ahead of him he saw a city
With tall buildings
Stretching skywards.
The falcon knew high places.
So he flew to the tallest building
And came to rest on a stone ledge near the top.

The falcon rested on the high ledge.
Slowly his strength returned.
So did his hunger.
His black eyes began searching this way and that.
On a nearby roof there was a large wire cage.
It was a coop where a man
Kept a flock of pigeons.

Every afternoon, the man came to the roof.
He opened the coop and allowed his pigeons
To circle about in the air.
The falcon watched the man let his pigeons loose
For their daily flight.
The falcon watched them with his deep-set eyes.
And then—
Spreading his mighty wings,
He left the ledge and entered the air.

High above the pigeons he wheeled,
Choosing his prey,
And for that moment the tired old hunter
Felt young and strong
And ruler of the sky again.
Then suddenly he dived.

Down, down he rushed.
Down in a great flash of speed,
Faster than the rushing wind!
Screaming the falcon hunting cry,
He pinned the pigeon with his powerful claws.
He struck once with his powerful beak.
The pigeon died quickly.

Finished with his meal,
The hunter returned to the high stone ledge.
He folded his wings,
And lowered his sharp beak.
But his black eyes stared straight ahead.
It was as if he were staring
Back into the past, to a time
When falcons were rulers of the skies.

Many, many years ago,
Men trained falcons to hunt.
Mighty kings and princes carried
The proud birds on their wrists.
The falcons were trained to hunt the skies,
Then dive swiftly to the kill.

In that time, when a sharp-eyed falcon
Wheeled high overhead,
No small animal was safe.
No fieldmouse, no rabbit, no bird.
This old falcon, too, had known
The wild swift flight
And the rush of the deadly dive.

But now,
For the falcon on the ledge,
Those days were gone, all gone.
It was as if, all at once,
Winter had rushed in on him.
Night closed over the city,
And the old hunter slept.

Many hours later the sun edged
Above the tall buildings,
And a new day began.
With morning the falcon's hunger returned.
But the pigeons were now safe
Inside their wire cage.
The old bird had to look elsewhere.

Far below, his black eyes saw a green park.
On the warm morning air,
The great bird circled hungrily.
He saw a fat grey squirrel run down a tree,
And rushed in for the kill.
But as the falcon clawed the squirrel,
A man walked by.
He picked up a large rock and threw it.

The rock found its mark.
The squirrel was safe.

Dropping the squirrel,
The falcon flew upward.
Slowly, slowly, he fought his way,
Back to the high stone ledge.
There he sat, his eyes half-closed,
His smooth head down.
Bright red blood ran down his wing,
Darkening the brown and white feathers.

Old and tired.
Old and tired.
In a little while the falcon forgot his hunger.
He even forgot his pain.
Once, in an earlier time,
A brave time when he was young and strong,
He had hunted all the skies,
Screaming the falcon hunting cry.
But
  Now,
    Now. . .

Later that day,
A passer-by
Found the falcon's thin body
Lying in the street.
The ruler of the skies was dead.

Seymour Reit

Lord Randal

'O where have you been, Lord Randal, my son?
O where have you been, my handsome young man?'—
  'I have been to the wild wood; mother, make my bed soon,
  For I'm weary with hunting, and fain would lie down.'

'Who gave you your dinner, Lord Randal, my son?
Who gave you your dinner, my handsome young man?'—
  'I dined with my sweetheart; mother, make my bed soon,
  For I'm weary with hunting, and fain would lie down.'

'What had you for dinner, Lord Randal, my son?
What had you for dinner, my handsome young man?'—
  'I had eels boiled in broth; mother, make my bed soon,
  For I'm weary with hunting, and fain would lie down.'

'And where are your bloodhounds, Lord Randal, my son?
And where are your bloodhounds, my handsome young man?'—
 'O they swelled and they died; mother, make my bed soon,
 For I'm weary with hunting, and fain would lie down.'

'O I fear you are poisoned, Lord Randal, my son!
O I fear you are poisoned, my handsome young man!—
 'O yes! I am poisoned; mother, make my bed soon,
 For I'm sick at the heart, and I fain would lie down.'

Anonymous

Activities

Lord Randal is a ballad or short story in verse.

Ballads are told in a quick, straightforward way without a lot of description.

They tend to deal with a small part of a longer story, and are about love, hatred, bravery, fighting, adventure and the supernatural.

Lord Randal uses a question and answer ballad form in which the son gives mysterious and worrying replies to his mother's questions. Finally, we discover that his lover has poisoned him.

Lord Randal started life as a spoken or oral ballad. It has no author (Anonymous) for it has been handed down over hundreds of years by singers and speakers who have changed it to suit their own tastes.

1 Tell the story of Lord Randal and his lover. What made her kill him?
2 Use the same question and answer method to write your own ballad.
 You might start like this:

 'O who did you meet . . ., my friend?
 O who did you meet, when walking your dog?'

A Snake Yarn

'You talk of snakes,' said Jack the Rat,
'But blow me, one hot summer,
I seen a thing that knocked me flat—
Fourteen foot long, or more than that.
It was a regular hummer!
Lay right along a sort of bog,
Just like a log!

'The ugly thing was lyin' there
And not a sign o' movin',
Give any man a nasty scare;
Seen nothing like it anywhere
Since I first started drovin'.
And yet it didn't scare my dog.
Looked like a log!

'I had to cross that bog, you see,
And bluey I was humpin';
But wonderin' what that thing could be
A-laying there in front o' me
I didn't feel like jumpin'.
Yet, though I shivered like a frog.
It *seemed* a log.

'I takes a leap and lands right on
The back of that there whopper!'
He stopped. We waited. Then Big Mac
Remarked, 'Well, then, what happened, Jack?'
'Not much,' said Jack, and drained his grog.
'It was a log!'

W T Goodge

A Swagman was an Australian ranch worker who travelled from one sheep station to another. Round the equipment (swag) that he carried he rolled his 'bluey', a grey-blue blanket.

Activities

Here is another poem with a part for everyone. It was written for the soundtrack of *Night Mail* (1936), a documentary film made by the GPO Film Unit which builds up an exciting pattern of images and sounds as a night mail train steams its way from London to Scotland.

The speaking parts should be organised as follows:

- CLASS .... everyone
- GROUPS A B C ...... three equal groups containing both girls and boys
- VOICES 1 — 21 ...... 21 solo speakers

Next, ask your teacher to read the poem aloud. Check the lines you will speak whilst this is being done.

Finally, rehearse the poem with the help and advice of your teacher.

When you can speak the poem well you might think of a public performance.

A video recording (24 minutes) is available on Cassette 6 from TEL Ltd, Knightsbridge House, 197 Knightsbridge, London SW7 1RB.

Night Mail

CLASS This is the night mail crossing the border,
Bringing the cheque and the postal order,
Letters for the rich, letters for the poor,
The shop at the corner and the girl next door.
Pulling up Beattock, a steady climb—
The gradient's against her, but she's on time.
Past cotton grass and moorland boulder
Shovelling white steam over her shoulder;
Snorting noisily as she passes
Silent miles of wind-bent grasses.

GROUP A Birds turn their heads as she approaches,
Stare from the bushes at her black-faced coaches.

GROUP B Sheep-dogs cannot turn her course,
They slumber on with paws across.

GROUP C In the farm she passes no one wakes,
But a jug in the bedroom gently shakes.

CLASS Dawn freshens, the climb is done.

GROUP A Down towards Glasgow she descends
Towards the steam tugs yelping down the glade of cranes,
Towards the fields of apparatus, the furnaces
Set on the dark plain like gigantic chessmen.

CLASS All Scotland waits for her:

GROUP B In the dark glens, beside the pale-green lochs
Men long for news.

SINGLE SPEAKERS: 1 Letters of thanks, (2) letters from banks,
3 Letters of joy from girl and boy,
4 Receipted bills and invitations
To inspect new stock or visit relations,
5 And applications for situations
6 And timid lovers' declarations
7 And gossip, gossip from all nations,
8 News circumstantial, (9) news financial,
10 Letters with holiday snaps to enlarge in,
11 Letters with faces scrawled in the margin,
12 Letters from uncles, cousins and aunts,
13 Letters to Scotland from the South of France,
14 Letters of condolence to Highlands and Lowlands,
15 Notes from overseas to Hebrides—
16 Written on paper of every hue,
17 The pink, the violet, the white and the blue,
18 The chatty, the catty, the boring, adoring,
19 The cold and official and the heart's out-pouring,
20 Clever, stupid, short and long,
21 The typed and the printed and the spelt all wrong.

CLASS Thousands are still asleep

GROUP A Dreaming of terrifying monsters,

GROUP B Or a friendly tea beside the band at Cranton's or Crawford's.

GROUP C Asleep in working Glasgow, asleep in well-set Edinburgh
Asleep in granite Aberdeen.

CLASS They continue their dreams;
But shall wake soon and long for letters,
And none will hear the postman's knock
Without a quickening of the heart,
For who can hear and feel himself forgotten?

W H Auden

SHORT STORY

Charles

The day Laurie started kindergarten he renounced corduroy overalls with bibs and began wearing blue jeans with a belt; I watched him go off the first morning with the older girl next door, seeing clearly that an era of my life was ended, my sweet-voiced nursery-school tot replaced by a long-trousered, swaggering character who forgot to stop at the corner and wave goodbye to me.

He came home the same way, the front door slamming open, his cap on the floor, and the voice suddenly became raucous shouting, 'Isn't anybody here?'

At lunch he spoke insolently to his father, spilled Jannie's milk, and remarked that his teacher said that we were not to take the name of the Lord in vain.

'How *was* school today?' I asked, elaborately casual.

'All right,' he said.

'Did you learn anything?' his father asked.

Laurie regarded his father coldly. 'I didn't learn nothing,' he said.

'Anything,' I said. 'Didn't learn anything.'

'The teacher spanked a boy, though,' Laurie said, addressing his bread and butter. 'For being fresh,' he added with his mouth full.

'What did he do?' I asked. 'Who was it?'

Laurie thought. 'It was Charles,' he said. 'He was fresh. The teacher spanked him and made him stand in a corner. He was awfully fresh.'

'What did he do?' I asked again, but Laurie slid off his chair, took a cookie, and left, while his father was still saying, 'See here, young man.'

The next day Laurie remarked at lunch, as soon as he sat down, 'Well, Charles was bad again today.' He grinned enormously and said, 'Today Charles hit the teacher.'

'Good heavens,' I said, mindful of the Lord's name, 'I suppose he got spanked again?'

'He sure did,' Laurie said. 'Look up,' he said to his father.

'What?' his father said, looking up.

'Look down,' Laurie said. 'Look at my thumb. Gee, you're dumb.' He began to laugh insanely.

'Why did Charles hit the teacher?' I asked quickly.

'Because she tried to make him colour with red crayons,' Laurie said. 'Charles wanted to colour with green crayons so he hit the teacher and she spanked him and said nobody play with Charles but everybody did.'

The third day—it was Wednesday of the first week—Charles bounced a seesaw onto the head of a little girl and made her bleed and the teacher made him stay inside all during recess. Thursday Charles had to stand in a corner during storytime because he kept pounding his feet on the floor. Friday Charles was deprived of blackboard privileges because he threw chalk.

On Saturday I remarked to my husband, 'Do you think kindergarten is too unsettling for Laurie? All this toughness and bad grammar, and this Charles boy sounds like such a bad influence.'

'It'll be all right,' my husband said reassuringly. 'Bound to be people like Charles in the world. Might as well meet them now as later.'

On Monday Laurie came home late, full of news. 'Charles,' he shouted as he came up the hill; I was waiting anxiously on the front steps. 'Charles,' Laurie yelled all the way up the hill, 'Charles was bad again.'

'Come right in,' I said, as soon as he came close enough. 'Lunch is waiting.'

'You know what Charles did?' he demanded, following me through the door. 'Charles yelled so in school they sent a boy in from first grade to tell the teacher she had to make Charles keep quiet, and so Charles had to stay after school. And so all the children stayed to watch him.'

'What did he do?' I asked.

'He just sat there,' Laurie said, climbing into his chair at the table. 'Hi Pop, y'old dust mop.'

'Charles had to stay after school today,' I told my husband. 'Everyone stayed with him.'

'What does this Charles look like?' my husband asked Laurie. 'What's his other name?'

'He's bigger than me,' Laurie said. 'And he doesn't have any wellies and he doesn't ever wear a jacket.'

Monday night was the first Parent-Teachers meeting, and only the fact that Jannie had a cold kept me from going; I wanted passionately to meet Charles's mother. On Tuesday Laurie remarked suddenly. 'Our teacher had a friend come see her in school today.'

'Charles's mother?' my husband and I asked simultaneously.

'Naaah,' Laurie said scornfully. 'It was a man who came and made us do exercises. Look.' He climbed down from his chair and squatted down and touched his toes. 'Like this,' he said. He got solemnly back into his chair and said, picking up his fork, 'Charles didn't even do exercises.'

'That's fine,' I said heartily. 'Didn't Charles want to do exercises?'

'Naaah,' Laurie said. 'Charles was so fresh to the teacher's friend he wasn't *let* do exercises.'

'Fresh again?' I said.

'He kicked the teacher's friend.' Laurie said. 'The teacher's friend told Charles to touch his toes like I just did and Charles kicked him.'

'What are they going to do about Charles, do you suppose?' Laurie's father asked him.

Laurie shrugged elaborately. 'Throw him out of the school, I guess,' he said.

Wednesday and Thursday were routine; Charles yelled during story hour and hit a boy in the stomach and made him cry. On Friday Charles stayed after school again and so did all the other children.

With the third week of kindergarten Charles was an institution in our family; Jannie was being a Charles when she cried all afternoon; Laurie did a Charles when he filled his wagon full of mud and pulled it through the kitchen; even my husband, when he caught his elbow in the telephone cord and pulled telephone, ash tray, and a bowl of flowers off the table, said, after the first minute, 'Looks like Charles.'

During the third and fourth weeks there seemed to be a reformation in Charles; Laurie reported grimly at lunch on Thursday of the third week, 'Charles was so good today the teacher gave him an apple.'

'What?' I said, and my husband added warily, 'You mean Charles?'

'Charles,' Laurie said. 'He gave the crayons around and he picked up the books afterward and the teacher said he was her helper.'

'What happened?' I asked incredulously.

'He was her helper, that's all,' Laurie said, and shrugged.

'Can this be true, about Charles?' I asked my husband that night. 'Can something like this happen?'

'Wait and see,' my husband said cynically. 'When you've got a Charles to deal with, this may mean he's only plotting.'

He seemed to be wrong. For over a week Charles was the teacher's helper; each day he handed things out and he picked things up; no one had to stay after school.

'The PTA meeting's next week again,' I told my husband one evening. 'I'm going to find Charles's mother there.'

'Ask her what happened to Charles,' my husband said. 'I'd like to know.'

'I'd like to know myself,' I said.

On Friday of that week things were back to normal. 'You know what Charles did today?' Laurie demanded at the lunch table, in a voice slightly awed. 'He told a little girl to say a word and she said it and the teacher washed her mouth out with soap and Charles laughed.'

'What word?' his father asked unwisely, and Laurie said, 'I'll have to whisper it to you, it's so bad.' He got down off his chair and went around to his father. His father bent his head down and Laurie whispered joyfully. His father's eyes widened.

'Did Charles tell the little girl to say *that*?' he asked respectfully.

'She said it *twice*,' Laurie said. 'Charles told her to say it *twice*.'

'What happened to Charles?' my husband asked.

'Nothing,' Laurie said. 'He was passing out the crayons.'

Monday morning Charles abandoned the little girl and said the evil word himself three or four times, getting his mouth washed out with soap each time. He also threw chalk.

My husband came to the door with me that evening as I set out for the PTA meeting. 'Invite her over for a cup of tea after the meeting,' he said. 'I want to get a look at her.'

'If only she's there,' I said prayerfully.

'She'll be there,' my husband said. 'I don't see how they could hold a PTA meeting without Charles's mother.'

At the meeting I sat restlessly, scanning each comfortable matronly face, trying to determine which one hid the secret of Charles. None of them looked to me haggard enough. No one stood up in the meeting and apologized for the way her son had been acting. No one mentioned Charles.

After the meeting I identified and sought out Laurie's kindergarten teacher. She had a plate with a cup of tea and a piece of chocolate cake; I had a plate with a cup of tea and a piece of marshmallow cake. We manoeuvred up to one another cautiously and smiled.

'I've been so anxious to meet you,' I said. 'I'm Laurie's mother.'

'We're all so interested in Laurie,' she said.

'Well, he certainly likes kindergarten,' I said. 'He talks about it all the time.'

'We had a little trouble adjusting, the first week or so,' she said primly, 'but now he's a fine little helper. With lapses, of course.'

'Laurie usually adjusts very quickly,' I said. 'I suppose this time it's Charles's influence.'

'Charles?'

'Yes,' I said, laughing, 'you must have your hands full in that kindergarten, with Charles.'

'Charles?' she said. 'We don't have any Charles in the kindergarten.'

Shirley Jackson

Understanding

1 Copy the layout on page 142 into your exercise book and then review *Charles*.

Your teacher is welcome to make other copies for your use.

SHORT STORY REVIEW

Title ______________________ Author ______________________

Who were the characters? ______________________

What were these characters like? ______________________

What happens in the story? ______________________

What did you enjoy or dislike about the story? ______________________

What is your star rating? * * * * * * * * * * best * worst

Rating ______________________

2 Make a list of the 'crimes' committed by Charles.
3 What kind of mother did Laurie have?
4 Was it just Laurie who had to stay after school or was it everyone?
5 Why did Laurie behave in the way he did?
6 What did Laurie's parents think of Charles?
7 Were Laurie's parents strict enough? Give reasons for your answer.
8 Why did Laurie turn into a helper?
9 Describe Laurie as his teacher saw him.
10 In which country does the story take place?
11 Was the teacher right in not telling Laurie's parents what was happening?
12 Give reasons for thinking that Laurie's behaviour was the same at home as at school.
13 Say in one sentence what this story is about.

Writing

14 Imagine you were one of Laurie's parents. What did you do when you realised there was no Charles?
15 Write a story about another dreadful child who wrecks the lives of other people.
16 Were you ever in a place you disliked? Tell how you behaved.
17 Tell of either your early days at nursery school or those of a younger sister or brother.

Discussion

18 Form groups of five or six and choose a chairman. Imagine the years have passed and Laurie is now your age. What kind of a boy has he become? Use the story to guide your discussion.
Share your views with the class when you have finished.

Bash Tchelik

A tsar had three sons and three daughters, and when he was dying, he told his sons that they should give their sisters in marriage to the first who might come for them.

He died, and shortly after the funeral there was a knocking at the palace gate, and a tearing of the air, and such disturbances of nature that the foundations of the palace quaked. Then came a voice.

'O princes, open the door!'

'Don't open!' cried the eldest brother.

'Don't!' said the second.

'I must open!' said the youngest. And he did so.

Something came in, but what it was the princes could not see, whether it was a fallen star or a coal of hell, and out of the dazzling brightness the voice spoke again.

'I have come for your eldest sister to take her for wife.'

'I will not give her,' said the first brother.

'I have no time to spare,' said the voice. 'I must take her now.'

'I will not,' said the second brother. 'How can I give my sister to one I can't see, and whom I do not know, nor can guess?'

But the youngest brother said, 'I will give her. Our father's last words were that we should do just this.' He took his sister gently by the hand, and led her towards the light. 'I hope that she will be a good wife.'

Lightning and thunder blinded and deafened the whole palace then, and when it had cleared, both the presence and the sister were gone.

And the next night a voice came again.

'O princes, open the door!'

They were too frightened to resist, and when the light stood on the floor it said, 'Give me your second sister.'

'I will not!' said the eldest brother.

'I will not,' said the second brother.

'I will,' said the youngest brother. 'It was our father's last wish on earth.'

And on the third night, 'O princes, open the door!'

'We will not give our sister by night,' said the first and second brothers together.

'I will,' said the youngest brother. 'May you have joy and happiness together.'

The next dawn all three princes decided to go out into the world to find their sisters, to be sure that they were happy and well. They travelled for many days until they lost their way in a dark forest, and at nightfall they looked for a place to camp, and they built their fire by the side of a lake. After they had eaten, they settled down to sleep, while the eldest prince kept watch.

At midnight the lake boiled, and the eldest prince saw a black hump driving a wave right for him. It was a water monster, but the prince fought it, and swung his sword through its head. He cut off the ears, and put them in a bag, then he threw the body into the lake and went to sleep.

The whole of the following day the brothers tramped through the forest until they came to another lake at sunset, and there they made a fire, and the second brother stood guard that night. And a monster attacked, as the other had done, but this one had two heads, which the brother split with his sword. He cut off both pairs of ears and put them in a bag, then he slept.

On the third night, by the third lake, the third brother watched, and the third water monster came, and it had three heads. The youngest brother killed the beast, and put three pairs of ears in a bag, and then he slept. Nor had any of the brothers mentioned any of the monsters to each other.

Now they left the forest behind them, and came into a fearsome desert, where the sun burnt them by day, and the winds chilled them by night. They built a fire of dead thorn bush, and while the two brothers made a shelter the youngest went off in search of wood for the fire.

He had not gone far when he came to the top of a rocky height, and below him he saw flames in a valley. He climbed down to beg wood of the people there, but when he came near he saw that the fire was burning in the mouth of a cave, and round the fire sat nine giants, roasting two men on spits. A cauldron seethed the limbs of more men, and there were long shapes hanging from hooks in the cave roof.

'Hello!' said the young prince, and he stepped forward into the light. 'I have been looking everywhere for you, my friends!'

The giants sized him up, but made no move. 'Welcome,' they said, 'since you are one of us. And since you are one of us, take a joint of this man now, eh? And then you will help us when we go a-foraging, eh?'

'By all means,' said the prince, 'and thank you.'

He joined the circle round the fire, and dipped his hand into the cauldron.

After this supper the giants said that they would have to go to find their breakfast before they slept, and the prince would come with them.

'Naturally,' said the prince. 'You will find a dwarf giant very useful, I promise.'

'We need not be long,' said the biggest giant. 'The city is not far away from which we have filled our larder these nineteen years.'

When they came to the city, the giants uprooted two pine trees, and put one against the wall. The prince, being small and light, went up the tree, and the giants then gave him the second tree to lean against the wall on the other side.

'I don't quite understand what it is you want me to do,' said the prince. 'Come and show me.'

So one of the giants climbed to the top of the wall, and propped the tree on the city side. The prince drew his sword in the shadow of the parapet, and when the giant bent forward to secure the tree against the wall, the prince took off his head with the sword, and pushed the body from the parapet into the dark of the street below.

'All clear,' he said to the giants outside the city, 'so up you come: one at a time, please, and don't rush. There's plenty for all.'

When the giants were headless, the prince went down into the city. He found the place empty.

But there was one light shining in the city. It came from a window at the top of a tall tower. The prince found the door and the stairway, and climbed to the room. It was furnished with silks and jewels, and on a bed of silver lay a beautiful girl, asleep.

The prince stood, watching, and as he watched, a snake slid through the window and on to the pillow and coiled itself to strike the girl. But the prince drew his dagger and threw it, taking the snake through the head, pinning it to the wall.

'Let no one be able to remove this dagger but me,' said the prince. He left the lighted room in the dark city and went back to the cave. There he burnt all that he found, and carried a load of wood to his brothers.

After they had slept and the day had come, they went on, and arrived at the city.

Now it was the habit of the tsar of this city to walk out each morning to view the havoc of the giants, and each morning there were fewer people between the giants' appetites and his only daughter's fair flesh. Yet if she had to be eaten, he would make certain that she was the last, and he had built her a tower, higher than giants could reach, with one stair, narrower than a giant's belly, and there she lived in safety. The giants would have to destroy the tower to reach her, and they would not do that while there were easier meals to be found.

Heavy with grief, the tsar walked about his city, and he entered the street where the pine tree stood against the wall—and there at its foot were tumbled nine headless bodies.

The people crept from their hiding places when they heard the great, joyful shout that the tsar gave, and soon the streets were alive with happiness. Then the snake was discovered, nailed to the wall by a dagger that no one could pull free.

The tsar issued a proclamation that the hero who had killed the giants and saved the life of the tsar's daughter would be honoured above all men, and would have the daughter's hand in marriage.

When the three brothers arrived at the inn by the city gate they found that all the talk was of high deeds, and they were asked if they had ever fallen in with adventures that had called for bravery.

'Well,' said the eldest brother, 'when we camped by the first lake on our way here through the forest, I stood guard while my brothers slept, and there came a water monster to eat us, but I killed it and cut off its ear.' And he opened his bag, and took out the proof of his tale.

'On the second night,' said the second brother, 'I was attacked by a monster with two heads, and these are the ears to show for it.'

'And on the third night,' said the youngest, 'I won my share,' and he tipped six ears out of his bag on to the table. 'Yet more than that,' said the prince, 'I know who sleeps in the silver bed, and I know what is hanging close by on the wall, and I can remove it.'

At this, the prince was taken to the presence of the tsar, who made him tell his story in every detail. Then he went to the girl's room in the tower, and lightly pulled the dagger from the wall and put it back in its sheath at his waist.

'You shall be my son,' said the tsar, and the prince and the tsar's daughter were married that night.

To the brothers the tsar offered castles, gold and land, but they said that they must continue with their search until they knew where their three sisters were kept and how they fared in the world, and so they rode away.

The prince and his princess were happy for a while, and then he too felt that he could not be at ease until he knew his sisters' fate. He said farewell to his tearful wife, but she called him back. Again he tried to leave, but now her father had heard of what he intended, and the tsar made him prisoner in the palace. He was honoured and loved, but he was not free.

One day, the tsar and all his court were to go hunting, and the prince was left alone with only the servants on duty to look after his needs and his custody. The prince was bored. The fine rooms and corridors were stale to him. He wandered down into the cellars, where he had never been.

The farthest passage of the farthest vaults was blocked with old wine casks. They had been there so long that their hoops had rusted away, their staves shrunk, and the prince soon cleared aside enough for him to see that the passage continued, even though the walls were crumbling with damp and age.

By the light of his lantern he saw a massive door at the end of the passage, and it was not long before he had made a space big enough for him to crawl through over the rotten barrels.

The door was rusted on its hinges, and was locked, but the prince found a key hanging against the wall under a mat of cobweb, and by using a splintered stave as a lever he managed to turn the lock and then to prise open the door.

The room inside was a dungeon of stifled air, and in the middle of the floor was a fountain of pure water which ran through a golden pipe into a golden basin, and near it a golden cup, rich in jewels and silver work.

But there was more in the dungeon. A man stood against the wall. His legs were bound in iron bands up to his knees, and his arms were bound in iron; and in each corner of the room there were chains fastened about oak beams, and each chain ran to an iron collar about the man's neck, so that he could not move any part of him. His hair and beard hid his face, and lay in the slime about his feet. The prince thought he must have been dead for centuries, but then he heard a whisper. 'Come to me. Do me a deed.'

The prince parted the hair over the man's face, and two eyes looked at him in the light.

'Give me water,' said the man, 'and I shall give you a life.'

The prince filled the golden cup and put it to the withered lips.

'What is your name?'

'Bash Tchelik,' said the man. 'Give me more water, and I shall give you another life.'

The prince refilled the golden cup.

'Another drink, for another life,' said the man, when the cup was empty.

'Very well,' said the prince, thinking that the prisoner was mad with his years of dark.

'Pour this one over my head,' said Bash Tchelik, and the prince did so.

Bash Tchelik lifted his arms, and the iron bands snapped like straw. He broke the collar about his neck with one twist. He kicked the iron from his legs. He grew. And as he stepped from the wall, the prince saw that there were great wings folded on his back.

Bash Tchelik went from the dungeon like a black storm, scattering the barrels in the passage, bursting the doors, and when the prince crawled from the cellar he found the palace wrecked and his wife stolen.

When the tsar returned from the hunt he did not blame the prince. 'You did not know this man,' he said. 'I have broken many an army on his lance, and he is not to be killed by any means.'

'If he breathes, he can be made to stop breathing,' said the prince. 'I shall seek him and destroy him.'

'Stay here,' said the tsar. 'I shall look on you as my son, now that I have no daughter, and I shall get you another wife. It is too late in my life for me to spend the years again in binding Bash Tchelik.'

'It is not too late in my life,' said the prince, and he took horse and left the palace.

He came to a castle, and from a window a girl called to him.

'Stay here, noble prince, and welcome, brother!'

He saw his eldest sister, and they laughed and wept together, and he entered the castle.

'My husband is the king of the dragons,' she said, 'and I am very happy. Our father must have known what was to happen, for the dying see the future, it is said, and you were the oldest in trust if not in years. Now you must go.'

'But why?' said the prince. 'I have only just this moment found you, and finding you was my first quest.'

'My husband has sworn that he will kill my brothers if he ever meets them again, because of the discourtesy he met with.'

'I shall stay,' said the prince.

'Then you must hide,' said his sister, and when the king of dragons came home, she asked him: 'Dearest husband, would you really kill my brothers if they appeared?'

'The first two,' said the king of dragons, 'I should roast. But the youngest I should welcome. So let him come out from hiding. I know he is here, for I smell human bones.'

The prince told the king of dragons about Bash Tchelik, and the king of dragons said, 'Be advised, and stay here with us. On the day that Bash Tchelik escaped from the tsar, I attacked him with five thousand of my dragons, and I managed to escape alive, but only just.'

'I must go,' said the prince.

'Then take this feather,' said the king of dragons, 'and if ever you need my help, burn it, and I shall be with you.'

The prince set out early the next day, and by evening he had reached the castle where his second sister lived. She was married to the king of eagles, and he too had promised to kill the brothers, except for the youngest, who had treated him graciously.

The prince stayed the night with his second sister and the king of eagles, and when he left, the king of eagles gave him a feather, to burn if he should need help.

And the third evening he came to the castle of the king of falcons, and found his youngest sister there, and the next day he took with him a feather from the king of falcons to strengthen him in his search for Bash Tchelik.

He found his wife in a mountain cave, alone, in rags, tending the fire. 'What work is this for a princess?' he said. 'Find me Bash Tchelik!'

'Run,' said his wife, 'before Bash Tchelik finds you. I have no power with him. I am his slave.'

'He shall die for that,' said the prince, and he put his wife before him on his horse, 'but first I shall take you to your father, to be safe while I kill this monster.'

He rode away, but there was only weeping from his wife, for she knew Bash Tchelik.

Bash Tchelik caught them before they had gone a mile, and he took the princess from the protection of her husband's sword as a badger takes honey from wild bees.

'Prince,' he said, 'you have stolen your wife. For that you must die. But I gave you a life, and now you have it.' And Bash Tchelik flew home to his cave.

Yet the prince did not let himself be beaten, and he went and took his wife again.

'Prince,' said Bash Tchelik, 'I gave you another life. You have it.'

But the prince went again and took his wife.

'Prince,' said Bash Tchelik, 'will you be shot with this arrow, or beheaded with this axe?'

'Neither,' said the prince. 'I choose my other life.'

'Remember it is the last,' said Bash Tchelik. 'The next one is your own.'

By now the prince had seen that no earthly weapon would harm Bash Tchelik, so he drew the three feathers from his pocket and burnt them. And at once the hosts of the dragon and the eagle and the falcon were with him, and they fell upon Bash Tchelik.

At the end of the day, the three kings flew unknown with the prince to safety.

'Our people are destroyed, and Bash Tchelik is not hurt,' they said. 'Give up your wife, since nothing can win her back.'

'I can win her,' said the prince, but this time he went cunningly, and whispered to his wife:

'All things that live can die. Find out the secrets of his life, and I shall lie close and listen.'

Bash Tchelik came home in the evening, and the princess said to him, 'Tell me where your life is hidden, so that I may guard it the better.'

Bash Tchelik laughed, and said, 'My life is in my axe.'

And when he came home the next day he found the princess kneeling before the axe, which she had draped with silk and adorned with spices.

Bash Tchelik laughed again. 'Why do you kneel here?' he said.

'I honour the power that can vanquish falcons and eagles and dragons,' said the princess.

'My life is not there,' said Bash Tchelik. 'It is in my bow.'

And the following day, the princess had decked the bow with fine ribbons.

'If I did not know that your husband lay dead upon my battlefield,' said Bash Tchelik, 'I should trust you the less, but none escaped: so you may know that far from here is a mountain of crystal, and in that mountain there lives a fox; and in that fox there is a raven; and in that raven there is an egg; and in that egg is my life.'

'Then I can sleep secure,' said the princess.

The prince went straight to the king of dragons, who took him on his back to the distant mountain, and with his fire he split the crystal, and the red fox that had shimmered like a ruby in its clear heart ran out. But the king of eagles pounced on it from the sky, and ripped the fur a darker red. Up sprang the raven, and fled on the wind, but the king of falcons closed with it, and the talons met on the raven's heart.

The king of falcons brought the raven to the prince.

Across the world, Bash Tchelik woke from his sleep, and sped roaring to the mountain. He found the prince by the broken crystal, fox and raven at his feet, and a smooth white egg in his hand.

The prince looked at Bash Tchelik. Bash Tchelik looked at the prince. The prince's fingers tightened on the egg. There was a tiny, splintered sound, and the shell was crazed with lines, faint as smoke. The fingers tightened. Yolk ran shining on his wrist.

Alan Garner

Understanding

1 How did the youngest brother differ from the other two?
2 Name four of the troubles that came to the three princes after they decided to go out into the world to find their sisters.
3 Tell in your own words how the nine giants were killed.
4 What made the tsar decide that his daugh-

ter should marry the youngest prince?

5 How many lives did Bash Tchelik give the prince in exchange for water?

6 Bash Tchelik looked like a man in the dungeon but there was one difference. What was that difference?

7 The husbands of the three sisters were all kings. Of what was each one the king?

8 Imagine you are a TV reporter. Give an on the spot broadcast of the tsar's morning walk.

9 Write three days in the diary of the youngest prince. Start with the day he went in search of wood for the fire.

10 You are the young prince and you suddenly realise that no earthly weapon could harm Bash Tchelik. You start 'thinking aloud' around the problem and how to solve it. Write down your thoughts.

11 Was the prince being cruel when at the end of the story he crushed the egg? Give reasons for your answer.

Writing

12 Imagine you are Bash Tchelik. Tell the story of your fight with the tsar, your capture and your years in prison.

13 Bash Tchelik did not stop the fingers of the prince tightening on the egg. When the yolk ran shining down the wrist of the prince was that the end of Bash Tchelik? Tell the story of what happened next.

The Wheelbarrow Boy

'Now see here, Thomis,' I said. 'I've just about had enough of you. If you haven't settled yourself down and started some work in two minutes' time I shall turn you into a wheelbarrow. I'm not warning you again.'

Of course, Thomis was not the only one: the whole class had the fidgets: he just happened to be the one I picked on. It was a windy day, and wind always upsets kids and makes them harder to handle. Also, I happened to know that Thomis' father had won a bit of money on the Pools, so it was easy to understand the boy's being off balance. But it's fatal to start making allowances for bad behaviour.

After about three minutes I called out, 'Well, Thomis? How many sums have you done?'

'I'm just writing the date,' said the boy sullenly.

'Right,' I said. 'You can't say I didn't warn you.' And I changed him into a wheelbarrow there and then—a bright red metal wheelbarrow with a pneumatic tyre.

The class went suddenly quiet, the way they do when you take a strong line, and during the next half-hour, we got a lot of work done. When the bell for morning break went I drove them all out so as to have the room to myself.

'All right, Thomis,' I said. 'You can change back now.'

Nothing happened.

I thought at first he was sulking, but after a while I began to think that something had gone seriously wrong. I went round to the Headmaster's office.

'Look,' I said. 'I just changed Thomis into a wheelbarrow and I can't get him back.'

'Oh,' said the Head and stared at the scattering of paper on his desk. 'Are you in a violent hurry about it?'

'No,' I said. 'It's a bit worrying, though.'

'Which is Thomis?'

'Scruffy little fellow—pasty-faced—always got a sniff and a mouthful of gum.'

'Red hair?'

'No, that's Sanderson. Black, and like a bird's nest.'

'Oh, yes, I've got him. Well now,' he looked at the clock. 'Suppose you bring this Thomis chap along here in about half an hour?'

'All right,' I said.

I was a bit thoughtful as I went upstairs to the Staff Room. Tongelow was brewing the tea, and as I looked at him I remembered that he had some sort of official position in the Union.

'How would it be if I paid my Union sub?' I said.

He put the teapot down gently. 'What've you done?' he asked. 'Pushed a kid out of a second-floor window?'

I pretended to be hurt. 'I just thought it was about time I paid,' I said. 'It doesn't do to get too much in arrears.'

In the end he took the money and gave me a receipt, and when I had tucked that away in my wallet I felt a lot better.

Back in my own room Thomis was still leaning up in his chair, red and awkward, a constant reproach to me. I could not start any serious work, so after about ten minutes I set the class something to keep them busy and then lifted Thomis down and wheeled him round to the Head.

'Oh, good,' he said. 'So the gardening requisition has started to come in at last.'

'No,' I said, dumping the barrow down in the middle of his carpet. 'This is Thomis. I told you . . .'

'Sorry,' he said. 'I'd clean forgotten. Leave him there and I'll get to work on him straight away. I'll send him back to you when he's presentable.'

I went back to my class and did a double period of composition, but no Thomis turned up. I thought the Old Man must have forgotten again, so when the bell went at twelve I took a peep into his room to jog his memory. He was on his knees on the carpet, jacket and tie off, with sweat pouring off his face. He got up weakly when he saw me.

'I've tried everything,' he said, 'and I can't budge him. Did you do anything unorthodox?'

'No,' I said. 'It was only a routine punishment.'

'I think you'd better ring the Union,' he said. 'Ask for Legal Aid —Maxstein's the lawyer—and see where you stand.'

'Do you mean we're stuck with this?' I said.

'You are,' said the Head. 'I should ring now, before they go to lunch.'

I got through to the Union in about ten minutes and luckily Maxstein was still there. He listened to my story, sighing now and then.

'You are a member, I suppose?'

'Oh yes,' I said.

'Paid up?'

'Certainly.'

'Good,' he said. 'Now let me see. I think I'd better ring you back in an hour or so. I've not had a case quite like this before, so I'll need to think about it.'

'Can't you give me a rough idea of how I stand?' I said.

'We're right behind you, of course,' said Maxstein. 'Free legal aid and all the rest of it. But . . . but I don't fancy your chances,' he said and rang off.

The afternoon dragged on, but there was no phone call from Maxstein. The Head got fed up with Thomis and had him wheeled out into the passage. At break-time I phoned the Union again.

'Sorry I didn't ring you,' said Maxstein when I got through to him again. 'I've been very busy.'

'What am I to do?' I asked.

'The whole thing,' said Maxstein, 'turns on the attitude of the parents. If they decide to prosecute I'll have to come down and work out some line of defence with you.'

'Meanwhile,' I said, 'Thomis is still a wheelbarrow.'

'Quite. Now here's what I suggest. Take him home tonight—yourself. See his people and try to get some idea of their attitude. You never know; they might be grateful.'

'Grateful?' I said.

'Well, there was that case in Glasgow—kid turned into a mincing machine—and the mother was as pleased as could be and refused to have him changed back. So go round and see, and let me know in the morning.'

'All right,' I said.

At four o'clock I waited behind and then, when the place was empty, wheeled Thomis out into the street.

I attracted quite a lot of attention on the way, from which I guessed the story must have preceded me. A lot of people I did not know nodded or said, 'Good evening,' and three or four ran out of shops to stare.

At last I reached the place and Mr Thomis opened the door. The house seemed to be full of people and noise, so I gathered it was a party in celebration of the Pools.

He stared at me in a glazed sort of way for a moment and then made a violent effort to concentrate.

'It's Teddy's teacher,' he bawled to those inside. 'You're just in time. Come in and have a spot of something.'

'Well, actually,' I said, 'I've come about Teddy . . .'

'It can wait,' said Mr Thomis. 'Come on in.'

'No, but it's serious,' I said. 'You see, I turned Teddy into a wheelbarrow this morning, and now . . .'

'Come and have a drink first,' he said urgently.

So I went in, and drank to the healths of Mr and Mrs Thomis. 'How much did you win?' I asked politely.

'Eleven thousand quid,' said Mr Thomis. 'What a lark, eh?'

'And now,' I said firmly, 'about Teddy.'

'Oh, this wheelbarrow caper,' said Thomis. 'We'll soon see about that.'

He dragged me outside into the yard and went up to the wheelbarrow. 'Is this him?' he said.

I nodded.

'Now look here, Teddy,' said Mr Thomis fiercely. 'Just you come to your senses this minute, or I'll bash the daylights out of you.' And as he spoke he began to unbuckle a heavy belt that was playing second fiddle to his braces.

The wheelbarrow changed back into Teddy Thomis and nipped smartly down the garden and through a hole in the fence.

'There you are,' said Mr Thomis. 'Trouble with you teachers is you're too soft with the kids. Here, come in and have another drink.'

Richard Parker

Understanding

1 Imagine you are Teddy. Explain your behaviour.
2 Tell the story of the boy in Glasgow.
3 Why did the Head wheel Thomis into the passage?
4 What kind of person was Teddy's teacher?
5 Why did the teacher attract attention when he pushed the wheelbarrow down the street to Teddy's home?
6 Describe Teddy's father.
7 How did Teddy's parents feel about him being a wheelbarrow?
8 What made the wheelbarrow change back into Teddy Thomis?
9 Which of these words best describes the story? Explain your choice of word.

unbelievable comic
supernatural romantic

10 Would you have liked to have been in Teddy's class?
Why, or why not?

Writing

11 Imagine the local newspaper followed up the teacher's story. Write in playscript form the interview between their reporter and the teacher, e.g.

REPORTER:
TEACHER:

12 Write your own school story about a pupil who resents the teacher.

Discussion

Form groups of five or six and choose a chairman.

13 Is it true that teachers are too soft with the kids? Base your discussion on group experience.

PLAYSCRIPT

Pantomime

Introduction

Pantomime is one of our great traditions.

To reach us it has had a long journey through the centuries.

It probably started with the Greeks who gave us the word *pantomimus* meaning 'player of every part' or 'I imitate all'. From the Romans came the idea of men dressing up as comic women and of girls dressing up as handsome heroes. France and Italy gave us the clowning, the pity, the tenderness and the animals, whilst popular songs and jokes were added by the British music hall.

The result is a hotch potch of romance, magic and farce: the unbelievable princes in fishnet tights, the sweet heroines, the bossy outrageous dames, the village simpletons, the barons without money, the fairy godmothers, the chorus girls, the glamorous costumes and scenery, the jokes, songs and audience participation.

The pantomime most often performed is that of Cinderella. It is the best-known fairy tale in the world and also one of the oldest. For over a thousand years the story of a young girl ill-treated by her stepsisters has been told and retold throughout Europe.

No one knows where the story came from, but we do know that it was first written down by Tuan Ch'eng-shih in China somewhere around the year AD 850. Many centuries later a Frenchman called Charles Perrault wrote a book containing all the stories his nurse had told him, and one of these was Cinderella. This book was translated into English by Robert Samber in 1729 and the plots of the stories used for spectacular entertainments in which famous music hall artists were able to introduce their own comic turns.

Pantomime has continued to adapt itself so that present day jokes go hand in hand with the story from the past. This you will see from the following script for a Cinderella pantomime shown on children's television.

Follow it word for word or alter it to suit yourselves.

Cinderella

Cast

In order of appearance

NARRATOR	the story teller
CINDERELLA	a young girl, dressed in rags
STEPMOTHER	Cinderella's stepmother
BUTTONS	a faithful servant and Cinderella's friend
TAPIOCA GORGONZOLA	the Ugly Sisters
FAIRY GODMOTHER	Cinderella's fairy godmother
PRINCE	Who invites everyone to a Ball at the Palace
MANWELLI	The Prince's incompetent manservant

Sets

1 The kitchen at Cinderella's home
2 A corner of the Great Hall at the Prince's Palace

Scene 1 Cinderella's kitchen early in the morning

The kitchen is a dark and gloomy place. Cinderella is just putting the finishing touches to the fire in the hearth. Then she begins to lay the table for breakfast. She is dressed in very old and tattered clothes. The narrator stands to one side of the stage . . .

NARRATOR Let me introduce you to our heroine, Cinderella. This is how her morning begins. Up at five every morning, clean out the grate, get the breakfast . . . Work, work, work from dawn to dusk. I really am going to get that girl to join a union. At least then she'll get teabreaks. But look out! Here comes the dragon—her stepmother, that is, now you'll see what we all have to put up with . . .

STEPMOTHER Is that table not set yet! The birds have been singing for hours, keeping me from my beauty sleep and not so much as a bowl of Snap Crackle and Pop on the table . . .

CINDERELLA Oh, but . . .

STEPMOTHER Don't give me any excuses, you're a lazy good-for-nothing, just like your father. I don't know why I ever married him, other than the fact that my two beautiful darlings needed a daddy to call their own.

NARRATOR Own! Their own *daddy* joined the Foreign Legion, just to get away from them!

STEPMOTHER Still, that's enough of that. Get that table finished and I'll go and call my darlings . . . (*exits, calling*) TAPIOCA! GORGONZOLA!

NARRATOR Voice like the Whitstable foghorn that woman, I don't know how Cinderella puts up with it. But shh! She's coming back.

STEPMOTHER (*pushing her two daughters along in front of her*) Come along you two, come along! You're not going to find husbands lying in bed all day and anyway you both need a good breakfast. Tapioca (*talking to her fat daughter*), you're looking quite peaky, dear, I think you'd better have two bowls of porridge, this morning!

TAPIOCA	(*sulking*) But I don't like porridge, it's all lumpy.
GORGONZOLA	Just the thing for you sister dear, it matches your figure!
TAPIOCA	Huh! You're only jealous, tin ribs! If it wasn't for your big head, you'd slip through the cracks in the floorboards . . .
STEPMOTHER	Girls! Girls! Sit down to breakfast this minute. (*They all begin to eat very noisily*)
NARRATOR	I reckon if they had a 'Hog of the Year Show', they'd have difficulty choosing between these two. But hang on, who's coming. Oh, it's only Cinderella's friend, Buttons . . .
BUTTONS	Excuse me, Madam. A messenger from the palace has just called with this. (*Buttons proffers a large message, rolled up and tied with ribbon*)
STEPMOTHER	(*snatching the message from Buttons*) Well, don't just stand there! Let me see it, let me see it!

TAPIOCA It's probably just a message to say that he's noticed my great beauty and he would like to marry me.

GORGONZOLA It's probably a message to say that he's noticed your great weight and he'd like you to visit his vineyards to tread his grapes.

STEPMOTHER Girls! Girls! Do stop squabbling and listen. It's an invitation to everyone in the house to attend a Grand Ball. The Prince has decided to marry and he is hoping to meet his future bride there.

GORGONZOLA Oh, how exciting, how spiffing, how, how . . . positively splendidiferous . . .

TAPIOCA Oh, do stop spitting and spluttering! Come on, we'll have to start our preparations now, if we're going to look our best!

BUTTONS (*muttering*) Polyfilla and plastic masks couldn't make *them* look any better! (*louder*) You said *everyone*, Madam. Does that mean that Cinderella and I can go to the Ball, too?

STEPMOTHER You! Go to the Ball! I can't believe you're serious. I'm sure the Prince has quite enough servants of his own! There will be lots of work for you two to do here. You'll be far too busy to go to the Ball! (*she sweeps out*)

CINDERELLA Never mind, Buttons, you tried. And anyway I'm sure we wouldn't really enjoy that silly ball. (*she looks disappointed*) And what would I wear? I haven't had a new dress since my silly father married that woman!

BUTTONS Oh, I don't mind for myself, Cinderella, only for you. I'm sure that the Prince would fall in love with you the moment he saw you.

End of Scene One

Scene 2 Cinderella's kitchen a few days later

NARRATOR You've no idea what it's been like this last few days! World War 3 would be like a Sunday School outing after this. Bring me! Fetch me! Carry me! And the arguing! Well, I've just had to cover my ears once or twice. How poor Cinderella has put up with them all, I just don't know. Oh no! Here they come again . . .

TAPIOCA But you promised! You said that if I was wearing the purple, you'd wear the orange or the green. If you wear that pink, we'll look like a bunch of grapes, seasick ones!

GORGONZOLA You only want me to wear the green because you know it doesn't suit my colouring . . .

TAPIOCA Colouring! Colouring! I've seen more colouring on a zebra crossing! You're just jealous of my beauty. Anyway, where's that wretched Cinderella, I've got a hundred things for her to do, I'm never going to be ready in time. CINDERELLA! CINDERELLA!
Enter Cinderella, looking harassed and overworked.

GORGONZOLA Have you filled the bath with goat's milk, as I instructed you?

CINDERELLA Yes, Gorgonzola.

TAPIOCA Don't bother taking the goats out. She'll never notice the difference the way she smells. And if you think I'm going in that dress you chose, you can think again. It makes me look like a pair of curtains . . .

GORGONZOLA Well, pull yourself together then!

The Ugly Sisters exit, still arguing. Buttons enters to find Cinderella crying.

BUTTONS Oh, don't cry, Cinders. I'm sure it will be a rotten old Ball anyway. Especially with those two and that old bat their mother, there.

CINDERELLA Oh, it's not really that, Buttons. It's just that I wish they could be a little bit kind to me sometimes. My father's so busy working to pay for their new hats and gowns, he doesn't have time to notice how horrid they are.

BUTTONS I know. It used to be so nice before they came to live here. I can't think what your father was thinking about when he married her, his mind must have been wandering.

CINDERELLA Yes, and I sometimes think that it has got lost altogether. (*they both laugh*)

BUTTONS Hush! I think I can hear them leaving at last . . .

TAPIOCA (*from offstage*) We must fly, we're going to be late!

BUTTONS (*pretending to shout*) Don't forget your broomsticks!

CINDERELLA (*laughs*)

BUTTONS That's better! You look much nicer when you laugh. In fact, you look happier altogether . . .

FAIRY GODMOTHER (*who has entered quietly, whilst they were talking*) I can make you happier still, Cinderella, if you will let me . . .

CINDERELLA Who are you? How long have you been there?

FAIRY GODMOTHER All your life, my dear, although you've never seen me before. But enough of that, do you want to go to this Ball or not?

CINDERELLA (*wistfully*) Yes, yes I would, but how? I've nothing to wear and I can't possibly get to the Palace now . . .

FAIRY GODMOTHER Just leave all of that up to me. Buttons, I'll need your help. Go out into the garden and pick the largest pumpkin that you can find. Beside it put six white mice.

BUTTONS (*offstage, pauses slightly then calls*) Yes, I've done everything. Oh! Oh! I don't believe it!

FAIRY GODMOTHER Now find me three black rats . . . (*she looks offstage*) Yes, those will do nicely. (*She waves her arms, as if to cast a magic spell.*) Perfect! You can look now, Cinderella.

CINDERELLA (*Cinderella looks offstage and gasps in amazement*) A gold coach drawn by six white horses! For me?

BUTTONS (*rushing in*) And a coachman in black livery, with two footmen at the back.

FAIRY GODMOTHER And now for you, my dear. It is time for your transformation. Come with me. (*Exit offstage, Cinderella meekly following her Godmother.*)

BUTTONS It's just like a dream, I can't believe it's happening. But I wonder where they've got to?

Buttons begins to pace the floor, pausing to peep offstage once or twice, until Cinderella reappears.

BUTTONS Oh, Cinderella, you look beautiful!

FAIRY GODMOTHER Hurry along now Cinderella, you're going to be very late. (*Cinderella rushes offstage.*)

CINDERELLA Goodbye, goodbye.

FAIRY GODMOTHER Don't forget Cinderella, you must be back by midnight. For as the clock chimes twelve my spell will end.

End of Scene Two

Scene 3 The Palace Grand Hall later that evening

NARRATOR Cinderella could hardly believe her good fortune. The Prince danced with her the whole evening. Tapioca and Gorgonzola were green with envy. In that green dress, Gorgonzola looked like the Jolly Green Giant!

CINDERELLA I . . . I really must be going soon. I haven't to be late home.

PRINCE Can't you stay a little longer? Just one more dance.

The clock begins to chime. Cinderella looks horrified. She rushes offstage, disappearing as the clock chimes twelve.

NO! NO! Stop! Bring her back someone. (*The Prince's manservant rushes after her, returning a moment later carrying a large black Wellington*) Manwelli, what is this?

MANWELLI A wellie, your lordship sir. (*Manwelli speaks with a foreign accent*) I found it on the steps, the young lady must have dropped it!

NARRATOR It's all to do with inflation, you know. Who can afford glass slippers, these days?

PRINCE Tomorrow I will take this slipper . . . er, I mean wellie to every house in the kingdom and whichever lady it fits, I will marry.

End of Scene Three

Scene 4 Back in Cinderella's kitchen the next day

TAPIOCA (*tapping her foot impatiently*) You'd think the Prince would be here by now, wouldn't you Mummy?

STEPMOTHER Patience my dear, patience.

GORGONZOLA I don't know what you're worrying about. Your shoes are like coal barges. Put wheels on them and you could do tours around the Widdecombe Rubbish Tips . . .

TAPIOCA That does it! (*She and Gorgonzola begin to fight. Then there is a loud knock at the door.*)

STEPMOTHER Stop it! Stop it at once. There's someone here. Tapioca! Pull in your stomach and try to look presentable. Gorgonzola, curl up your toes, that way you might just get on that boot!

BUTTONS (*entering with the Prince and Manwelli. Manwelli has the boot on a cushion*) His Royal Highness.

Everyone bows to the Prince.

PRINCE (*looking doubtfully at the Ugly Sisters*) Erm, (*coughs loudly*) yours is the last house in the kingdom and I haven't found anyone who the boot fits.

TAPIOCA Let me try it, Your Highness. I'm sure I won't disappoint you.

The Prince pulls a face and then looks relieved as Tapioca gives up struggling to get the boot on.

GORGONZOLA Perhaps if you tried the G fitting, my dear. (*She glances in a superior way at her sister*) Let me try it on, my feet have always been much daintier than yours. (*She removes her shoe with a flourish*)

TAPIOCA Now you know why they call her *Gorgonzola*!

She struggles hard, but she cannot make the boot fit.

PRINCE What are we to do, Manwelli, will I never have a matching set?

BUTTONS Do not despair, Your Majesty. There is still one person who has not tried on the boot. (*Buttons goes offstage and returns with Cinderella*)

PRINCE (*looking at Cinderella closely*) Will you try on the boot?

CINDERELLA (*nodding meekly*) Yes, Your Royal Highness. (*The boot slips on easily*)

PRINCE My love!

CINDERELLA My Prince! (*they embrace*)

THE UGLY SISTERS UGH! My heart! (*The Ugly Sisters fall in a heap, clutching their hearts*)

NARRATOR And they all lived happily ever after. Well nearly all of them . . . and at least for part of the time . . .

The End

Questions

1 Cinderella has been called 'a sweet, dreamy person'. Is this true? Is she sweet? What are her dreams?

2 Show from the pantomime that Cinderella has:

a timid father
a stepmother who never stops nagging
two bad-tempered and quarrelsome sisters

3 Imagine you were Buttons at the wedding of the Prince and Cinderella. How would you feel? Were you fairly treated?

4 Was Cinderella a money-grabber who just wanted to get away from her stepmother and stepsisters?

5 Are Cinderella and her Prince people with real emotions who live, love and suffer? Or are they just two dolls in a glass case?

6 'Their own daddy joined the Foreign Legion, just to get away from them.' Give a short description of the father of the Ugly Sisters as you would imagine him to be.

Group work

7 *Scripting* (1)
Form groups of five or six.
You have been asked to make the pantomime longer for a public performance.
Discuss the idea of introducing ONE of the following as a new scene.
(a) Twelve dwarfs who jump out of the clock at midnight at the Ball
or
(b) A lightning tour of several countries by the Prince in his search for Cinderella
Write the script (the way in which conversation is written down in a play) needed for this extra scene.
Copy the layout used on pages 158–163 and don't forget to include any necessary stage directions, e.g. (*The Ugly Sisters fall in a heap, clutching their hearts*).

8 *Scripting* (2)
Form groups of five or six.
Write a different ending for the pantomime in which Cinderella stays faithful to Buttons.
One idea would be for the Prince to notice that a ring Buttons is wearing once belonged to his long-lost elder brother and Buttons turns out to be that brother.
Cinderella could then get away from her home and marry Buttons the Prince.

9 *Playmaking*
Form groups of three or four.
Select one of the characters in the pantomime for discussion.

How would the character speak, dress and behave?
Make rough sketches to show how the character would move on the two sets (see page 158).
Create space in the classroom so that you can share with others the ideas you have for acting your character.

Kaleidoscope

10 • How did Cinderella wear a glass slipper without breaking it and cutting her foot?
The truth is the the slipper was not glass at all. It was made of fur.
The mix-up came when the story was translated from French into English.
The French words for her slipper were '*pantoufle en vair*' meaning 'slipper of fur or sable', but this was translated as '*pantoufle en verre*' or 'slipper of glass'.
One of the great mistranslations in the history of literature!

- If you are good at drawing, make a sketch of the ballroom scene (see page 162) as you would like to see it staged.
- Prokofiev (1891–1953) was a Russian composer who wrote music for a ballet about the Cinderella story (*Cinderella*, Op. 87). Listen to a recording of his music and think about what you hear and see in it.
- Watch the videotape of the film *The Slipper and the Rose* and then discuss it. This is an updated version of the Cinderella and Prince Charming story with Richard Chamberlain as the Prince and Gemma Craven as Cinderella. The tape may be obtained from:
Iver Film Services Ltd,
Pinewood Studios,
Iver,
Buckinghamshire SLO ONH
Tel: 0753 651700

The mumming play

Introduction

It is possible that this is the oldest play in the world.

In different shapes and forms it is found in Europe, Africa and the Americas. In this country there was a mumming play in many counties, and even villages had a play which had been altered to suit the actors it could find.

Wherever it was performed, the play had a simple plot. There was a fight between two people and one of them was killed. A doctor was called in and the dead person brought back to life with a pill or a bottle of medicine.

It is easy to see that this is a play about death and of rising from that death. In fact, it was about an old year dying and a new one beginning. As such it was performed in the winter months when there was little sun, nothing growing, and the times were hard.

In one county the mummers, their faces blacked as a disguise, went round the villages at Christmas time calling at the inns and acting their play. Disguise was important, especially for the dancers, for they were the magic men, the witch doctors, and like witch doctors they had to wear a mask. Should they be recognised, the spell would be broken, and the new year would never rise from the death of winter.

Costumes were of the simplest kind, for villagers had little money to spend. There might be a top hat, a soldier's helmet, paper frills, streamers pinned to clothes, and dangling ribbons of bright colours. The swords were wooden strips with cross-pieces, or even walking sticks.

As with pantomine there was room for many characters. Parts were given to extra soldiers and dancers and to any odd or strange people. In one county a man dressed as a woman was an important part of the play.

Until recent times the mumming play was performed, mainly at Christmas time, by folk actors all over Britain and Ireland. Today it survives in very few places.

When you read or act this play remember that you are present at a custom that is older than you can ever imagine.

Christmas Mummer's Play

Song begins outside. Then Mummers dance in singing: as they come in they form a circle. Each has his sword over his right shoulder and the man behind takes hold of the sword of the man in front of him. The Fool comes behind the tallest man and pretends that he cannot reach his sword-point—plays the fool with it. Song ended they stand back and at once Enter Father Christmas, who walks forward and then round in a ring.

FATHER CHRISTMAS Here come I, Old Father Christmas.
Welcome or welcome not
I hope Old Father Christmas
Will never be forgot.
My head is white, my back is bent,
My knees are weak, my strength is spent.
Nineteen hundred and sixty—
Is a very great age for me.
And if I had been growing all these years
What a monster I should be.

FOOL An old man indeed thou must be,
And thou seemest but three score and three.

FATHER CHRISTMAS (*Pushing Fool aside*)
A room, a room, a gallant room,
And give us room to rhyme,
We've come to show activity
Upon this Christmas time.
Acting youth or acting age,
The like was never seen upon this stage. (*Stands back*)

FOOL Room, room, brave gallants, give us room to sport.
For to this room we wish now to resort.
(*Swings bladder at audience and performers*)

(*Enter Sweep*)

SWEEP Sweep, sweep a room for me
And all our jolly company.
Sweep, sweep,—a sweep am I
Will sweep for one and all right merrily.
(*Sings*) Oh, my name it is Jack Hall, chimney sweep,
Oh, my name it is Jack Hall, chimney sweep,

Oh, my name it is Jack Hall, and I've robbed both great and small,
And my neck shall pay for all when I die, when I die.

I have twenty pound in store, that's no joke,
I have twenty pound in store, that's no joke,
I have twenty pound in store, and I'll rob for twenty more,
And my neck shall pay for all when I die, when I die.

Oh they tell me that in jail I shall die,
Oh they tell me that in jail I shall die,
Oh they tell me that in jail I shall drink no more brown ale.
And my neck shall pay for all when I die, when I die.

Up the ladder I did grope, that's no joke,
Up the ladder I did grope, that's no joke,
Up the ladder I did grope, and the hangman spread the rope.
Oh, but never a word said I coming down, coming down.

FOOL Come, come, thou sweep,
Enough of thee.
(*Enter St George for all to see*)
Now St George, thou champion bold,
Thou has fought much as I've been told.
If that be true, pray tell us now
Where thou hast fought, and when, and how?

ST GEORGE (*Swaggers round*)
Here comes I, St George, the valiant man,
With my broad sword and spear in hand,
Who fought the Dragon and brought him to the slaughter,
And for this won the King of Egypt's daughter.
What man or mortal before me dares to stand
I'll cut him down with this deadly hand.
I'll slay him and cut him as small as flies
And send him to Jamaica to make mince pies.

(*Enter Turkish Knight, who should be as tall as possible*)
TURKISH KNIGHT Here come I, the Turkish Knight,
In Turkish Land I learnt to fight.
I'll fight St George with courage bold
And if his blood is hot, I'll run it cold.
(*Fiercely as possible*)

ST GEORGE Tut, tut, thou little fellow!
Thy talk is very bold;
Just like those little Turks
As I've been told.
If thou be a Turkish Knight.
Pull out thy sword and fight!
Or pull out thy purse and pay
For I'll have satisfaction
Before I go away.

TURKISH KNIGHT St George, St George! Thou dost not well to boast.
The Knight of Turkey is my name,
And by my sharp sword at my side
I hope to win the game.
My body's lined with lead,
My head is made of steel,
So to battle, to battle, let thee and I try
To see which on the ground shall lie.
(*They fight furiously. Onlookers cheer, some one, some the other. The Turkish Knight falls*)

ST GEORGE O Ladies and Gentlemens, you see what I have done,
I've struck this Turk down like the Evening Sun!

FATHER CHRISTMAS Fear not, I have a little bottle by me side,
In it hocum, slocum, a liquid spar,
I'll touch his eyes, nose, mouth, and chin,
And say 'Rise, dead man' and he'll fight again.
(Turk leaps up ready to fight, and they go at it again, even more furiously. Turk again falls, and lies quite stiff)

(Enter Moll Finney)

MOLL St George, St George, what has thou done?
Thou has surely ruined thyself
By killing my only son. *(Kneels beside Turk)*
Is there a doctor to be found
Can cure a man lies bleeding on the ground?

FOOL *(Running round)*
Doctor, doctor, come and see,
This man is wounded in the knee.
Doctor, doctor, come and try,
This man is wounded in the thigh.
Doctor, doctor, do thy part,
This man is wounded in the heart.

(Enter Doctor)

DOCTOR I be the noble Doctor Good.
And with my skill I'll stop his blood;
My fee's *ten* pound, but only *five* if I
Don't raise this man alive.

FOOL What canst do then, Doctor?

MOLL Doctor, doctor, cure this man.

DOCTOR No. I see he's too far gone.

MOLL *(weeping)* Then walk in, Jack Vinney.

(Enter Jack Vinney to left of body)

JACK VINNEY My name is not Jack Vinney,
My name is Mr John Vinney,
A man of fame,
Come from Spain,
Do more than any man again.

DOCTOR What canst thou do, Jack?

JACK VINNEY Cure a magpie with the toothache.

FOOL How do that then, Doctor?

DOCTOR Cut his head off and throw his body in the ditch.—
Any fool could do that.

JACK VINNEY Thou callst me a Fool, dost thou?

FOOL Now cheer up, Jack, don't get thee crusty.

JACK VINNEY Take care you Fool, or I'll chop thee as fine as dust,
And send thee to make mince-pie crust.

DOCTOR (*Drags Fool away, and signs Jack to the body*)
Now, Jack, cure this man.

JACK VINNEY Give me my spectacles.
(*He is handed a huge pair of wooden spectacles*)
Now give me my pliars.
(*He is handed great pliars – makes great to-do and finally produces a huge horse's tooth*)
Here's a tooth enough to kill any man
But he will cure this man.
(*Turk is pulled up and shakes Jack's hand*)

JACK VINNEY I come from Spain,
Thou comes from France,
Call in the Morris Men,
Let's have a dance.
(*Morris men come forward and dance 'Shepherd's Hey' with crossed swords. When this is over, St George and Turkish Knight come forward*)

TURKISH KNIGHT St George, St George, pardon me, pardon me,
And from this country give me leave to flee.

ST GEORGE Go home. Go home. Thou curly Turkish Knight,
Go back to thine own land
And learn to fight:
Tell them all across the sea
We'll fight a thousand men like thee.

FOOL St George, thou speakest very bold,
And hast good cause as I've been told.

ST GEORGE Here am I, St George, in shining armour bright,
I am a famous champion,
Likewise a worthy knight:
Seven long years in a close cave was kept,
And out of that into a prison leapt.
Many a giant did I subdue
And fought the fiery dragon too.
First I fought in France
Second I fought in Spain
And now I've come to Kempsford*
The Dragon to fight again.
(*Stands back to right*)

DRAGON Stand on head, stand on feet,
Meat, meat, meat, for to eat!

* Or wherever you are performing the play.

I am the Dragon, here are my jaws
I am the Dragon, here are my claws.
Meat, meat, meat, for to eat.

Stand on head, stand on feet.
(*Snaps at all performers, who draw back in terror*)

FOOL (*Dodges to side of St George*)
Now champion bold knocked down the Turkish Knight,
Make haste to kill the dragon in the fight.

ST GEORGE Should twenty thousand Dragons rise,
I'd fight them all before your eyes.
And now I'll slay the Dragon – my wonders to begin,
A fell and fiery dragon he, but I will clip his wing.
(*They fight, onlookers cheer them on. St George falls. Right Hand, St George's man, rushes to help and supports him against his knee*)

RIGHT HAND Alack, alack, my master he has slain,
Send tell the doctor he must come again.

DOCTOR Here come I, the Doctor Good,
I'll stop the noble Champion's blood.

RIGHT HAND Pray, Doctor, where do you come from?

DOCTOR I come from Portugal, France, and Spain,
To fetch dead people to life again.

RIGHT HAND Pray, noble doctor, what can you cure?

DOCTOR I have some pills
To cure all ills,
Hard corns, soft corns, any corns that be,
The itch, the stitch, the palsy and the gout,
Pains within and pains without,
And any old woman that's been dead seven year,
If she's got one tooth left to crack one of these here.
(*Holds up box and shakes it to rattle the pills, finally opens it, takes out a huge pill and stuffs it into St George's mouth*)

DOCTOR Rise up, St George, and fight again
And may the Dragon yet be slain.
(*They fight again—at last Dragon falls dead*)

ST GEORGE (*Exhausted but triumphant, on one knee*)
Now I have killed the Dragon and brought him to the slaughter.

FOOL (*Pretending to hunt for someone*)
Alas, where is the King of Egypt's daughter?

ST GEORGE Long ago she died and lies at rest
But still I fight to succour the opprest.

FATHER CHRISTMAS St George, thou hast the Dragon slain again,
With thy brave hand his life is nobly ta'en.

TANNER Away from here his body carry fast
First go his feet and then his head come last.

ALL Which is his head? Is this it? Is that it?
(*Dragon carried out feet first*)

(*Enter Big Head*)
BIG HEAD In comes I, as ha'n't been hit
With my big head, and little wit,
My head's so big and my wit's so small,
Come in Humpty Jack to please them all.
(*Some of the actors dance 'Bacca Pipe's Jig' over swords*)

(*Enter Beelzebub*)
BEELZEBUB In comes I, Beelzebub,
In my hand I carries a club;
And in my hand a warming pan.
And don't you think
I'm a merry old man?

(*Enter Humpty Jack*)
HUMPTY JACK Here comes I, little Humpty Jack,
Wife and family on my back
Out of nine I haven't but five.
And half of them are starved alive.
The roads are dirty and our shoes are bad.
So please put *something* into our bag,
Ladies and Gents our play is ended
Our money box is recommended.

Beelzebub goes round with the box while other actors sing 'Good King Wenceslas'. Morris off, with Dragon too, to 'Maid o' the Mill'. Twice round room and out, Fool coming last, fooling to the end.

Anonymous

Part of fourteenth-century manuscript illustrating some of the animal masks and costumes worn by mummers at Christmas at the court of Edward III

Questions

1 What happens outside the house before the mummers enter?
2 How does the Fool make his entrance?
3 What does the Fool use to make people stand back and provide an acting space?
4 Who is the first character to enter when everything is ready?
5 What prize was given to St George for killing the Dragon?
6 Why does the Turkish Knight have to be as tall as possible?
7 With what does Father Christmas raise the Turkish Knight from the dead?
8 What is the relationship between Moll Finney and St George?
9 Why was Doctor Good unable to cure the Turkish Knight?
10 How did Jack Vinney cure a magpie with the toothache?
11 What is pulled from the mouth of the Turkish Knight with pliars?
12 What happens to the Turkish Knight after the sword dance *Shepherd's Hey* is over?
13 How does the Dragon make the other performers draw back in terror?
14 Who supports St George when he is wounded by the Dragon?
15 With what does Doctor Good cure St George?
16 Why was the Fool pretending to hunt for the King of Egypt's daughter?
17 What is the job of a Tanner? Why does a Tanner take away the body of the Dragon?
18 Why is Humpty Jack brought into the play?
19 What is happening whilst the actors sing *Good King Wenceslas*?
20 How do the mummers make their exit?

Group work

21 *Playreading*
Break up into groups of seven for playreading.
Each member of the group to read two parts as there are fourteen characters in the play.
Take parts and then look over lines before reading.
Make sure you know:

the moods of your characters
when to pause, and
when to come in quickly at the end of a previous speech

Rehearse the play and then present your readings in turn to the class.

Kaleidoscope

22
- The Morris Dance was brought to England in the reign of Edward III (1312–1377). In it the dance bells were jangled and staves or swords clashed. It was a military dance of the Moors in which five men and a boy took part. The boy wore a head-piece called a *morione* and he was known as *Mad Morion*. How *Mad Morion* became the *Maid Marion* who lived with Robin Hood in Sherwood Forest is another story. Try to find out more about Morris Dancing from a local group.
- The animal called a dragon is a winged crocodile with a snake's tail. In the Middle Ages priests used the dragon to represent sin and those who followed pagan gods. The Church therefore has a number of dragon slayers — St George, St Michael, St Clements and St Margaret — who fought and overcame sin. If there is a church near you named after one of these saints it may have a dragon in one of its stained-glass windows.
- St George is supposed to have killed his dragon on *Dragon's Hill* in Berkshire. There is a bare place on the hill where nothing will grow, and that is where the blood of the dragon ran out. Find out what really happened on that hill by using the names *Cedric* (founder of the West Saxon kingdom) and *Naud* (a Welsh chieftain) as clues.

Index

Acknowledgements

We are grateful to the following for permission to reproduce copyright material:

George Allen & Unwin for the poem 'A Small Dragon' from *Notes to the Hurrying Man* by Brian Patten; the author, Michael Baldwin for an extract from *Grandad With Snails* (pub Routledge & Kegan Paul); The Bodley Head for the poem 'A Snake Yarn' by W T Goodge from *The Poetry Makers Book 2* ed James McGrath, and an extract from *Minerva's Stepchild* by Helen Forrester; Jonathan Cape Ltd on behalf of the Executors of the W H Davies Estate for the poem 'Leisure' from *The Complete Poems of W H Davies*; the author's agents for the poem 'My Mother Saw a Dancing Bear' from *Figgie Hobbin* by Charles Causley (pub Macmillan); Gerald Duckworth & Co Ltd for the poem 'Winter and the Huntsman' from *Selected Poems Old and New* by Osbert Sitwell; Faber and Faber Ltd for the poems 'Night Mail' from *Collected Poems* by W H Auden, 'Take One Home for the Kiddies' from *The Whitsun Weddings* by Philip Larkin, 'Preludes' from *Collected Poems 1909–1962* by T S Eliot; The Folio Society Ltd for an extract from *The Exeter Riddle Book* trans Kevin Crossley-Holland (pub by The Folio Society Ltd for its members, 1978); Hamish Hamilton Ltd for the story 'Bash Tchelik' by Alan Garner from *The Hamish Hamilton Book of Goblins* ed Alan Garner; Henry Holt and Co Inc for the poem 'Steam Shovel' from *Upper Pastures* by Charles Malam Copyright 1930, © 1958 by Charles Malam; Mr R Howard for the poem 'The Knifesmith' by Dorothy Howard from *My Kind of Verse* ed John Smith; the author's agents for the story 'Charles' by Shirley Jackson from *The Lottery and Other Stories* (pub Farrar, Strauss and Giroux Inc) Copyright 1943, 1949 by Shirley Jackson; Michael Joseph Ltd for an extract from *The Country Diary of an Edwardian Lady* by Edith Holden (first pub in Great Britain by Michael Joseph/Webb & Bower) Copyright © Richard Webb Ltd 1977; the author, Norman MacCaig and the Hogarth Press for the poems 'Frogs' from *Surroundings* and 'A Summer Farm' from *Riding Lights*; the author's agents for the poem 'The Fight of the Year' from *Watchwords* by Roger McGough; John Murray (Publishers) Ltd for the poem 'Hunter Trials' from *Collected Poems* by John Betjeman; the author's agents on behalf of the author for the story *The Wheelbarrow Boy* by Richard Parker; The James Reeves Estate for the poem 'Mr Kartoffel' from *James Reeves The Complete Poems* © James Reeves Estate; Rigby Publishers, Adelaide for the poem 'Autumn Leaves' by Robyn Marsack from *Youth Writes Again* ed Marcia Kirsten; the author, Ian Serraillier for the poem 'The Two Ravens' from *I'll Tell You a Tale* © Ian Serraillier 1973, 1976 Longman Group & Puffin Books; The Society of Authors as the literary representative of the Estate of John Masefield for the poem 'Cargoes'.

We have been unable to trace the copyright holders in the Review of 'The Turbulent Term of Tyke Tiler' by Gene Kemp from p B28 *Bookpage* 3rd Issue 1980, the story 'Cinderella' from *Crackerjack Annual* 1982, 'Early Memories' by Alfred Marks from *Next Move* (BBC Publications/Belmont Press), and would appreciate any information that would enable us to do so.

Picture Acknowledgements

We are grateful to the following for permission to reproduce photographs and other copyright material;

Associated Press, page 57 below (photo Philip Whitley); BBC Hulton Picture Library, pages 84 and 91; British Museum, page 172; Lance Browne, page 57 above; Ron Chapman, page 18; Croyde Area Residents Association, page 8; Faber and Faber, *The Turbulent Term of Tyke Tiler*, page 105 (illustration by Carolyn Dinan); Sally and Richard Greenhill, pages 19 below, 61, 62 and 85; Hammersmith and Fulham Archives, page 93; India Book House Publishers, Bombay, pages 43–8; Michael Joseph, *The Country Diary of an Edwardian Lady*, page 87; Frank Lane Picture Agency, pages 35 (photo Walter Jarchow) and 89 (photo Arthur Christiansen); Sheelah Latham, page 19 above; *Longman New Generation Dictionary*, pages 3 and 4; Mansell Collection, pages 125 and 166; Mary Evans Picture Library, pages 13 and 73 (courtesy of the Estate of W. Heath Robinson); Methuen, *Thelwell's Complete Guide to Equitation*, 1962, page 127; Photosource, page 76 (photo Keystone); Sefton Picture Library, pages 25, 26, and 100; Sport and General, page 55; Times Newspapers, pages 37 and 38; Topham, pages 30 (photo Keystone), 40 (photo J. Allan Cash), 50 (photo Press Association), 68 (photo R. Sheridan) and 159 (photo Central Press); Victoria and Albert Museum, page 168; John Walmsley, page 41; Warburg Institute, University of London, page 22; World Wildlife Fund, page 99.

Cover photograph by Presse Sports, Paris.